Mary Lamson Clarke

The Star Crystal Cook Book

Mary Lamson Clarke

The Star Crystal Cook Book

ISBN/EAN: 9783744788755

Printed in Europe, USA, Canada, Australia, Japan

Cover: Foto ©Lupo / pixelio.de

More available books at **www.hansebooks.com**

STAR CRYSTAL

COOK BOOK.

EDITED BY

MISS MARY L. CLARKE.

PRINCIPAL MILWAUKEE COOKING SCHOOL.

PRICE 50 CENTS.

1890.
PUBLISHED BY
J. G. FLINT, MILWAUKEE.

COPYRIGHT, 1890, BY J. G. FLINT.

PREFACE.

In the multitude of cook-books of all degrees of excellence the only excuse for another must be found in its meeting a want often felt though not always recognized.

This little work brings together in convenient form a few of the most desirable recipes from many standard authorities.

The compiler is especially indebted to Mrs. Lincoln's Boston Cook-Book, Miss Parloa's Kitchen Companion, Délice's Franco-American Cookery Book, and Filipini's admirable chapter on Sauces in "The Table."

For recipes both new and old, grateful acknowledgements are also due to the many friends and pupils who have generously shared their manuscript treasures, some of which are now printed for the first time.

May "The Star Crystal Cook Book" find its place in many kitchens for daily reference and prove a daily helper.

MARY L. CLARKE.

NOTE.—The recipes marked S. are furnished by Mr. Ernest Schafer, cook at the White House during the administration of Pres. Garfield, and since then a *chef* in one of the leading hotels of the Northwest.

TABLE OF EQUIVALENTS.

A speck makes one-quarter saltspoonful.
Ten eggs, average size, make one pound.
Four saltspoonfuls make one teaspoonful.
One-half ounce bottle extract makes 12 teaspoonfuls.
Three teaspoonfuls make one tablespoonful.
Eight tablespoonfuls of dry or solid materials make 1 cup.
Sixteen tablespoonfuls of liquid material make 1 cup.
Two gills make 1 cup.
One wine glass makes one-half gill.
One cup contains eight ounces of liquid.
One tablespoonful butter makes one ounce.
One tablespoonful granulated sugar makes one ounce.
One heaped tablespoonful powdered sugar makes one ounce.
One tablespoonful flour makes one-half ounce.
Two tablespoonfuls ground spice make one ounce.
Five nutmegs make one ounce.
One quart sifted pastry flour makes one pound.
One quart less one gill, sifted patent flour makes one pound.
One scant pint granulated sugar makes one pound.
One pint butter makes one pound.
One pint chopped meat, packed, makes one pound.
One cup rice makes one-half pound.
One cup cornmeal makes six ounces.
One cup stemmed raisins makes six ounces.
One cup cleaned currants makes six ounces.
One cup stale bread crumbs makes two ounces.

TABLE OF PROPORTIONS.

One quart of flour requires one pint of butter, or butter and lard mixed for pastry.

One quart of flour requires one heaping tablespoonful of butter for biscuit.

One quart of flour requires two tablespoonfuls of butter for shortcakes.

One quart of flour requires one cup of butter for cup cakes.

One quart of flour requires one-half level teaspoonful of salt.

One quart of flour requires three teaspoonfuls of Star Crystal Baking Powder.

One quart of flour requires one pint of milk for muffins, gems, etc.

One quart of flour requires one scant quart of milk for batters of all kinds.

One measure of liquid to three measures flour for bread.

One teaspoonful of soda to one pint of sour milk.

One teaspoonful of soda to one cup of molasses.

One teaspoonful of salt to one pound of meat.

A spoonful means that the material should lie as much above the edge of the spoon as the bowl sinks below it. A heaping teaspoonful means that the material should lie twice as high above the edge of the spoon as the bowl sinks below it. A level teaspoonful should hold 60 drops of water. All dry materials are measured after sifting

A spoonful of salt, pepper, soda, spice is a level spoonful.

One-half of a spoonful is measured by dividing through the middle lengthwise.

A speck is what can be placed within a quarter inch square surface.

HOW TO MAKE BREAD.

Sift seven pounds of flour in a deep pan, make a hole in the center of the flour, into which pour one quart of warm water, in which has been dissolved one cake of good yeast.

Beat the mixture well with a large spoon, cover with flour and set to rise in a warm place; in two hours it will be ready for kneading.

Dissolve a handful of salt in about three pints of warm water, with which make the whole into a soft dough, knead well with your hands and set to rise for two or three hours. Then work and make into loaves, set to rise again about two hours and then bake in a good hot oven. This will make nine loaves of bread.

S.

WATER BREAD, NO. 2.

One quart patent flour, sifted, one-half teaspoonful salt, one-half teaspoonful sugar, one level tablespoonful butter or lard, one-quarter ounce compressed yeast dissolved in one-half cup tepid water, one pint warm water. Measure flour, sugar and salt into a six-quart mixing-bowl. Pour hot water enough to dissolve it onto the shortening, then add cold water to make just one pint of water at the right temperature (about 80 degrees), mix in the dissolved yeast and make a batter with the flour, beating well.

Add more flour till the mixture is stiff enough to handle on the moulding board; knead hard and long, not less than twenty minutes, using as little flour as possible to keep it from sticking. Remember that a soft sponge makes a much more delicate, tender bread that will keep moist longer than a hard, stiff sponge.

Cover closely with cloth and tin cover, and let rise till it doubles its bulk. Cut it down and let rise again; divide into four parts and shape into round loaves putting two in each pan, or shape part as biscuit. Cover and let rise to double its bulk. Bake in a hot oven about forty-five minutes. Take from the pans as soon as done and wrap in a thick cloth used for no other purpose. Lay on a rack to cool and turn the baking pans over them to secure a thin papery crust. A large stone jar is the best thing to keep bread in, and loaves must not be put away until entirely cold.

MILK BREAD, WITH A SPONGE.

Pour one pint of scalding milk on one tablespoonful each of butter and sugar and one-half teaspoonful salt; when lukewarm add one-quarter cup yeast (one-half cup if mixed in the morning). Stir in three and one-half cups of flour and beat well. Let it rise over night or till very light, then add enough more flour to kneail and work it till smooth and fine grained. Let it rise in the bowl, cutting down two or three times. This makes an excellent rule for tea-biscuit, Parker-House and other rolls, and by doubling the measure of butter and adding the white of an egg well beaten, you have the delicious White Mountain rolls.

GRAHAM BREAD.

One pint milk, scalded and cooled, two tablespoonfuls brown sugar, one-half teaspoonful salt, one-quarter ounce yeast dissolved in one-half cup water, sifted Graham meal enough to make a dough as stiff as can be beaten with a wooden spoon— about six cups. Mix in the order given and beat till smooth; let rise very light, then with knife and spoon shape into loaves in the pans, let rise again to double its bulk. Bake in a less hot oven than is needed for white bread, and a little longer.

STEAMED BROWN BREAD.

Two cups rye meal, one cup corn meal, one-third cup molasses, one teaspoonful salt, one teaspoonful soda dissolved in two tablespoonfuls water, one pint sour milk, steam four hours.

VIENNA ROLLS.

One pint of milk, half a cup of home made yeast, flour enough to make a stiff batter, rise over night, in the morning add one egg, one tablespoonful of butter and flour enough to make it stiff to roll, mix well and let rise, then knead it again, roll out, cut with a round tin and fold over; put in a pan, and cover very close, let them rise again until they are very light, and bake in hot oven. S.

GRAHAM BREAD, NO. 2.

Two cups of buttermilk, one-half cup of best syrup, one teaspoonful of soda, one-half teaspoonful of salt, stir with a spoon to a stiff mass (not too stiff), put it into a three pint or a two quart basin well buttered, put into a steamer over cold water which gives the loaf more time to rise; steam about one hour, then place in the oven, and give it a brown color. S.

GRAHAM BISCUITS.

One pound of flour, one and one-half teaspoonfuls of Star Crystal Baking Powder, one egg, two tablespoonfuls of butter, two of sugar, mix light and add milk enough to make a stiff dough, cut out with a cutter and bake in a moderate oven. S.

CRACKERS.

One cup of buttermilk, one-half a cup of butter and four eggs; knead hard, pound the dough until like honey comb. S.

BAKING POWDER BISCUIT.

One quart sifted flour, one teaspoonful salt, three rounded teaspoonfuls Star Crystal Baking Powder, two tablespoonfuls butter, enough cold milk to make a stiff dough (patent flour will require about one pint). Mix all the dry materials, then rub in the butter with the fingers until the whole is fine as meal, add the milk gradually, mixing and cutting through with a knife till the whole is a light spongy mass. Turn on a well-floured board and press out with the hands to three-fourths of an inch thick, cut in rather small rounds and bake at once in a very hot oven.

TWIN BISCUIT.

Make as above and roll only one-half as thick. Spread the rounds with soft butter, put two together and bake quick.

GRAHAM GEMS.

Two coffee cups graham meal, one pint cold water mixed well together at night. Next morning add one tablespoonful butter, melted, one level teaspoonful salt, two heaping teaspoonfuls Star Crystal Baking Powder. Put into heated gem irons and bake twenty minutes in a hot oven.　　　　S.

WHITE-HOUSE TEA BISCUITS.

To one and one-half quarts of flour add three heaping teaspoonfuls of Star Crystal Baking Powder, sift well, rub six ounces of best butter into the flour as fine as possible, add cold milk enough to make a short dough, mix light with a spoon (do not use hands for mixing) roll out to the thickness of an inch, cut out with a small cutter, sprinkle the top with well-beaten yolk of an egg, and bake rather quick.　　S.

RICH BREAKFAST MUFFINS.

One quart of flour, three heaping teaspoonfuls of Star Crystal Baking Powder, two eggs, one or two tablespoonfuls of butter, one pint of milk, one-half cup of sugar. Mix thoroughly, drop into well-greased forms and bake in a hot oven.　　S.

MUFFINS, NO. 1.

One pint of flour, two teaspoonfuls Star Crystal Baking Powder, one cup milk, two eggs, one-half teaspoonful salt, one tablespoonful butter, melted, mix flour, baking powder, and salt together, beat the eggs to a cream, add the milk to them and mix with the flour to a smooth paste. Lastly, beat in the melted butter and bake in buttered muffin pans about thirty minutes.

MUFFINS NO. 2, ENGLISH MUFFINS.

One quart of flour, 1 teaspoonful salt, one-third cake (one ounce cake) compressed yeast, one and one-half cup of warm water. Dissolve the yeast in one-third cup of cold water, add it with the salt and the warm water and gradually stir it into the flour. Beat the dough thoroughly; cover and let rise in a warm place until spongy, about five hours. Then shape the dough on a floured board into balls about twice as large as an egg. Flatten to one-third of an inch thick. Lay these on a warm griddle which has been lightly greased and set on the back of the stove to rise slowly. As soon as they have risen a little draw them forward and cook slowly, turning often.

They should take about twenty minutes to rise and fifteen minutes to bake. Tear them apart and butter them while hot.

Miss Parloa.

PLAIN MUFFINS NO. 3.

One quart of flour, half a cup of butter melted, one egg, a quarter of a cup of sugar, two cups of milk, two heaping teaspoonfuls of Star Crystal Baking Powder, a pinch of salt, mixed well and bake in a quick oven in muffin rings.

RYE BREAKFAST MUFFINS.

One cup rye meal, one cup flour, one cup milk, one-quarter cup sugar, one-half teaspoonful salt, two teaspoonfuls Star Crystal Baking Powder, one egg well beaten. Mix all the dry materials. Add milk to the beaten egg and beat well together. Bake twenty minutes in muffin tins in a quick oven.

JOLLY BOYS.

Add another egg to the above mixture and milk enough to drop by teaspoonfuls into hot fat; or, they are delicious to omit the sugar and eat them hot with maple syrup for breakfast.

RYE MUFFINS, NO. 2.

One-half teaspoonful soda, one-half teaspoonful salt, one cup sour cream, one cup rye flour, one tablespoonful sugar, one cup wheat flour. Roll rather thin on a baking sheet, split and serve with cream and salt, or pour thickened milk as for milk toast, over it.

ROYAL MUFFINS.

Two cups "cerealine," three cups flour, one pint milk, three teaspoonfuls Star Crystal Baking Powder, one-half teaspoonful salt, two eggs, one tablespoonful butter. Sift flour, sugar, salt and baking powder together; add "cerealine," the milk and beaten eggs; lastly the butter, melted, beat hard for two minutes, fill muffin pans two-thirds full and bake about twenty minutes in *hot* oven.

CORN MUFFINS.

One cup corn-meal, two tablespoonfuls sugar, one teaspoonful salt, one even tablespoonful butter, five cups boiling water. At night mix the meal, salt, sugar, in top of double boiler; add the boiling water and butter and cook one hour. Turn into a mixing bowl and pour over it one-quarter cup water to keep a crust from forming. In the morning beat it up soft and smooth, mix one and one-half cups fine yellow corn flour, one and one-half cups white flour, two even teaspoonfuls Star Crystal Baking Powder and stir into the mixture. Add one egg well beaten, bake in iron gem pans in a hot oven; *or*, in the morning add one cup each of corn, rye and wheat flour; *or*, one and one-half corn, one graham, one-half cup wheat flour. These are good enough to pay for the extra trouble of cooking the evening before using. This rule makes fifteen muffins.   BOSTON COOK BOOK.

CORN BREAD.

One quart of sweet milk, corn-meal enough to thicken, three eggs, half a cup of butter, two tablespoonfuls of brown sugar, two heaping teaspoonfuls of Star Crystal Baking Powder and bake in a hot oven.   S.

SPONGE CORN BREAD.

One cup flour, two eggs well beaten, one-half cup of corn-meal, one and one quarter cups milk, one-half teaspoonful salt, one teaspoonful butter, melted, two teaspoonfuls Star Crystal Baking Powder. Mix in order given and bake in a shallow round pan, or square cake tin.   BOSTON COOK BOOK.

CORN AND RICE CAKES.

One pint white corn-meal, one teaspoonful salt, one tablespoonful flour, one cup cold boiled rice, one egg well beaten, one pint of milk, one tablespoonful melted butter, two heaping teaspoonfuls Star Crystal Baking Powder, bake in muffin pans about twenty minutes.

HOMINY AND CORN MEAL CAKES.

Mix two tablespoonfuls fine uncooked hominy, one-half teaspoonful salt, one tablespoonful butter, one-half cup of boiling water. Set over the boiling teakettle till the water is all absorbed, pour one cup boiling milk on one scant cup of cornmeal, add two tablespoonfuls sugar and the hominy, cool and whisk in two eggs (yolks and whites beaten separately), one heaping teaspoonful Star Crystal Baking Powder. Bake in gem pans twenty minutes.   BOSTON COOK BOOK.

PEARLED CORN MEAL CAKE.

One cup N. Y. Health Food Co.'s pearled corn-meal, one-half cup flour, one tablespoonful sugar, one teaspoonful salt, two teaspoonfuls Star Crystal Baking Powder, two eggs, one cup sweet milk, one tablespoonful butter, melted. Mix in order given, bake about one-half inch thick, in a rather quick oven.

THIN CORN CAKE.

One cup corn-meal (yellow), one-quarter teaspoonful salt, one round tablespoonful butter, one-half cup *boiling* water, one teaspoonful sugar. Pour the boiling water on meal, sugar and salt. Beat thoroughly. Add the butter and when well mixed spread very thin on buttered tin sheets. Bake slowly about twenty minutes.

QUICK SALLY LUNN.

One quart flour, one teaspoonful salt, three teaspoonfuls Star Crystal Baking Powder, three eggs well beaten with two tablespoonfuls sugar, one pint milk, one heaping tablespoonful butter softened enough to beat it. Beat very smooth; makes two square pans.

QUICK COFFEE BREAD.

Same as above, using five eggs and sprinkling sugar on top with a little cinnamon, instead of mixing it with the dough.

MARGERY DAW'S TEA CAKES.

One cup milk, one pint flour, three eggs, butter the size of an egg, three teaspoonfuls Star Crystal Baking Powder. Bake twenty minutes in muffin pans.

BLUEBERRY·TEA CAKE.

One quart flour, one teaspoonful salt, and two of Star Crystal Baking Powder sifted with the flour. One cup sugar, two eggs, one pint sweet milk, one-half cup butter, melted, beat all well together; then add one pint blue-berries or huckle-berries that have been picked over and well dusted with flour. Stir carefully, not to break the berries. Fill pans about three-quarters full and bake about one-half an hour in a moderate oven. Serve with stewed berries. MRS. HELEN CAMPBELL.

SQUASH MUFFINS

One pint flour, two teaspoonfuls Star Crystal Baking Powder, two eggs, one teaspoonful salt, four tablespoonfuls sugar, two cups sifted squash, and milk enough to make a drop batter (about 1 cup). Bake like Tea Cakes.

GERMAN PANCAKES.

Two cups of flour, two eggs, one teaspoonful Star Crystal Baking Powder, sift well, a little salt, one cup of milk, beat altogether well, not too thin and fry in hot butter. Use small frying pan.
S.

FRENCH PANCAKES.

Two cups flour, three eggs, one heaping teaspoonful Star Crystal Baking Powder, a little salt, one cup of milk. Beat well together for five minutes and fry in hot butter, roll up and fill with any kind of fruit, sprinkle a little powdered sugar over the top and serve hot.   S.

PLAIN WHEAT CAKES.

Make a batter with one quart of flour, two heaping teaspoonfuls Star Crystal Baking Powder well sifted, add milk enough to smoothen, beat two eggs, one-half cup of melted butter, a little salt, mix well and bake on hot griddle.   S.

PANCAKES, NO. 2.

Beat three eggs with a pint of milk, add a pinch of salt, one teaspoonful Star Crystal Baking Powder and sufficient flour to make it into a smooth batter, fry them in hot butter, roll them over on each side, drain and serve very hot with lemon and sugar.
    S.

PANCAKES, NO. 3.

One pint flour, one teaspoonful salt, two teaspoonfuls Star Crystal Baking Powder, three eggs well beaten, butter the size of an egg, melted and beaten in with two cups of milk.

The griddle should never be greased, but rubbed smooth with brown paper and salt, and should be hot enough to hiss as the batter is poured on it. Bake till full of fine holes, then turn and bake on other side till it falls a little. Pancakes should not be turned the second time.

WAFFLES, NO. 1.

Using the above mixture with only one and one-quarter cups of milk makes a batter right for cooking in waffle irons. If sour cream can be had, omit the butter and Baking Powder, using one teaspoonful soda instead.

INDIAN WAFFLES.

One-half cup Indian meal, one tablespoonful butter and two cups boiling milk. Beat smooth and set away to cool. When cool, add two eggs, one round cup of flour, one teaspoonful Star Crystal Baking Powder, one-half teaspoonful salt, bake as usual.

RAISED WAFFLES, NO. 2.

One pint milk, one and one-half pints flour, one egg, one teaspoonful salt, one-quarter ounce compressed yeast dissolved in two tablespoonfuls tepid water. Beat all well together and let rise, covered, for four hours. Cook as above.   S.

RICE WAFFLES.

Stir one cup warm boiled rice into the first mixture for waffles and bake as before.

WAFFLES, NO. 3.

Beat carefully into one quart of flour, one quart of sweet milk, one cup of melted butter, and one-half teaspoonful salt, a half cup of home-made yeast. When raised add two eggs, beat them well and let rise again. When light enough bake in hot waffle irons and sprinkle a little sugar over them.

SHORT CAKE, NO. 1.

(For Strawberries or Peaches.)

One quart flour, one teaspoonful salt, three teaspoonfuls Star Crystal Baking Powder sifted with it, rub in one-half cup butter and one-half cup lard, one and one-quarter cup milk. Bake in two long biscuit tins, marking off in squares before baking. Bake in a very quick oven till a good brown. Use a generous quart of fruit for each layer, dusting thick with powdered sugar. Pile whipped cream on the top layer just before serving.

SHORT CAKE, NO. 2.

One pint flour, one-half teaspoonful salt, two teaspoonfuls Star Crystal Baking Powder sifted together, one-quarter cup

BREAD, ETC. 17

butter rubbed in, one egg, one scant cup milk. Bake one-half inch thick.

SHORT CAKE, NO. 3.

Beat 3 eggs very light (not less than ten minutes of rapid beating) add one and one-half cups sugar, one-half cup cold water, two cups pastry flour, two teaspoonfuls Star Crystal Baking Powder. Whisk very quickly together and bake in three jelly-cake tins about ten minutes.

RYE SHORT CAKE.

One pint rye meal, one teaspoonful salt, one pint wheat flour, one tablespoonful lard well rubbed in, three heaping teaspoonfuls Star Crystal Baking Powder, sweet milk enough to roll out. Bake one inch thick on a tin sheet for about forty minutes.

APPLE DUMPLINGS, NO. 1.

Fill a two quart granite ware pan two-thirds full of tart apples, pared, quartered and cored, add one-half cup water, cover and set on stove to cook while preparing crust; mix well together one quart flour, one teaspoonful salt, three teaspoonfuls Star Crystal Baking Powder, one-half cup butter rubbed into the flour till fine as meal. Add enough sweet milk to make a dough as soft as can be handled easily. Roll out to exactly fit the pan, cut several gashes to let the steam escape; lay it over the hot apples and cover with a deep pie plate. Cook on top of the stove for half an hour, setting the pan on a trivet if necessary to keep the apple from burning. Then lift the cover and brown the crust in a hot oven. Serve with hard sauce.

APPLE DUMPLINGS, NO. 2.

Make biscuit crust as in No. 1, but add flour to roll out. Core and quarter two large apples; roll each quarter in a small piece of crust and lay in a well buttered biscuit tin. Dot them with bits of butter and sprinkle over two tablespoonfuls of sugar. Set the tin into the oven and pour on boiling water to nearly cover. Bake about thirty minutes in an oven hot enough to have them browned in that time.

PEACH COBBLER.

Prepare a rich short cake crust, using cream to mix it if possible. Fill a granite baking dish about one-half full with pared and stoned peaches. Allow one quart sugar to each quart of fruit. Cover and bake for an hour or longer until the peaches show a dark red color. Cool and serve with sugar and cream.

DOUGHNUTS, NO. 1.

One-half cup sugar, two eggs, one tablespoonful melted butter, one saucespoonful salt, beaten well together. Add one-half cup milk and two cups flour in which has been sifted two teaspoonfuls Star Crystal Baking Powder. If not stiff enough to roll, knead in more flour.

DOUGHNUTS, NO. 2.

One heaping cup of sugar, one quart flour, one-half teaspoonful cinnamon, three teaspoonfuls Star Crystal Baking Powder, one-half teaspoonful salt, two eggs, wet with milk enough to roll out and shape. It will take a little more than one cup. Fry in fat enough to brown them in about two minutes.

RAISED DOUGHNUTS.

One pint milk scalded and cooled, one cup of sugar, one saltspoonful salt, one-half cup butter, two-thirds cup yeast, one egg, one-half a nutmeg. Flour to knead like bread but rather soft. Rise six to eight hours, then roll and cut in shape, rise again and fry.

CRULLERS.

One-half cup butter, one cup sugar, two eggs, one teaspoonful Star Crystal Baking Powder and as much flour as can be worked in with a spoon, one teaspoonful essence of lemon. Cut in thin strips and plait them, fry very dry in moderately hot fat.

S.

GINGER CRULLERS.

One cup New Orleans molasses, two eggs, one-half cup sweet milk, one tablespoonful melted butter, one teaspoonful each of ginger and cinnamon, two teaspoonfuls Star Crystal Baking Powder, one teaspoonful salt, flour to roll as soft as can be easily handled. Fry as usual and roll in powdered sugar as soon as done. CREOLE COOK BOOK.

SOUR MILK DOUGHNUTS.

Two eggs beaten light, one cup sugar, one cup sour cream, four cups flour, one-half teaspoonful soda, one teaspoonful each of cinnamon and salt. Have board well floured and take on it one large spoonful of dough, kneading gently till firm enough to roll out and cut. Mix the trimmings with a fresh spoonful and roll again, repeating until all are used. Cook in fat hot enough to make them rise instantly to the top. MRS. HENDERSON.

FRITTER BATTER.

Two eggs beaten smooth, one cup flour, one-half teaspoonful Star Crystal Baking Powder, one-half cup milk, one teaspoonful salt, one tablespoonful salad oil. Beat with Dover beater till glossy and smooth. If intended for fruit add one teaspoonful sugar.

PINEAPPLE FRITTERS.

Cut the fruit in thin small sections; dip each in the batter and fry a handsome brown. Serve with sauce made by boiling the juice of the pineapple with one-half cup sugar, and adding one tablespoonful Curaçoa to it just before serving.

SHADDOCK FRITTERS.

Make batter as before, using the juice of the fruit instead of milk. Tear the pulp in small bits and mix well through the whole. Be careful not to let any of the white fibre get into the pulp.

OYSTER FRITTERS.

Pick over and parboil the oysters; drain them well and use their liquor in place of milk to mix in the batter, adding more salt and pepper if needed.

BRAIN FRITTERS.

Clean the brain, removing the red membrane and clots of blood if there are any. Soak in cold salted water one hour. Then put them into one pint cold water with tablespoonful lemon juice and one-half teaspoonful salt. Bring to boil as soon as possible, boil gently ten minutes then plunge into cold water until wanted. Dry gently on a soft cloth; cut into sections convenient for serving; roll each in fritter batter, which should be made a trifle stiffer than for the other dishes. Drop into hot fat and fry a handsome brown. Drain each piece on clean brown paper in a warm oven before serving. Have ready some stalks of parsley washed and dried. Plunge these into the hot fat for one minute until they become crisp, but do not let them lose their color. Serve on a folded napkin, dressing with the crisp parsley.

VEGETABLE FRITTERS.

Vegetables of any kind should be thoroughly cooked, drained and either chopped fine or cut in pieces convenient for serving before being added to the batter.

CHICKEN FRITTERS.

One cup chicken-stock, one heaping tablespoonful flour, one tablespoonful butter, one-half teaspoonful salt, one-half teaspoonful celery salt, one cup cold chicken. Mix the flour smoothly in the hot butter, add the boiling stock gradually and when smooth, the seasoning, let simmer till quite thick. Pour half the sauce onto a small platter, and spread the chopped chicken evenly over the top. Then cover with the remainder of the sauce. Place on ice and when cold and hard cut into inch by two inch pieces. Dip them quickly into fritter batter and fry in deep, hot fat.   Mrs. D. A. Lincoln.

GERMAN FLOUR DUMPLINGS.

One and one-half quart flour, two teaspoonfuls Star Crystal Baking Powder, mix well through a sieve beat two eggs and add cold water enough to make a stiff dough, set in a cool place for two hours, cut out with a spoon, and boil in salt water for twenty minutes. S.

GERMAN TOAST.

Cut one-half inch slices of stale bread, soak them each side in milk enough to soften, then dip in beaten egg, roll in cracker dust and fry in hot lard, and serve with cream sauce. S.

POTATO DUMPLINGS.

Boil one dozen potatoes, peel and set them to cool. When cold break them into a bowl, add six well beaten eggs, a little nutmeg, salt, pepper, one cup of flour and work it to a stiff dough, form into round balls and boil in salt water about twenty minutes. S.

ADDITIONAL RECIPES.

ADDITIONAL RECIPES.

ADDITIONAL RECIPES.

Hints on the Easiest Way in Cake Making.

Make ready all the materials before beginning to put any cake together; that is, see that flour, butter and sugar are weighed or measured as the receipt calls for. Let the fire be in good condition to finish baking without putting on fresh coal. If the fire is too hot, discourage it by leaving the griddles open for five minutes or less, then sprinkle on a little fresh coal without increasing the draft. Leave the oven doors open a few minutes before putting in a sponge cake, if it is still too fierce If too hot on top, set a pan of cold water on the grate above the cake, never lay a paper over it. Thin cakes need a hotter oven than loaves and should bake in ten minutes; sheets of cake in from fifteen minutes to one-half hour; loaves from one-half hour to an hour, while fruit cake will require from two to four hours. Do not attempt to bake a fruit cake weighing over fifteen pounds in an ordinary stove oven. Send it to some first-class baker unless you are so fortunate as to have an old-fashioned brick oven in your house. Whatever kind of cake you are baking, divide the time into quarters; during the first quarter it should not change except by rising; during the second it should finish rising and begin to brown; during the third and fourth finish browning, settle a very little and shrink from the pan. On first taking from the oven, set for a few minutes on a stove hearth or shelf where you can barely hold your hand. A very light, delicate cake will fall if cooled too quickly, or shaken while hot.

Pans should be greased with sweet lard or unsalted beef fat, as butter scorches so easily; line them with paper and grease the paper very little, if the paper is thin, not at all. In baking pound or fruit cake line the pan with more than one thickness of paper, on the bottom there may be as many as six, but in such cases only the layer of paper next to the cake needs to be greased.

Mix cake in an earthen bowl and always with a wooden spoon (or the hand). Use only best materials; it is better to go without cake than try to make it, or eat it when made with "cooking" butter, second rate eggs or low grade baking powders.

Coarse texture with large holes shows insufficient beating and too large a measure of baking powder. Brown sugar may be used for fruit cake, but finest granulated (or sifted) is the best. Coarse granulated sugar makes heavy cake with a hard sticky crust, powdered sugar makes a tight, close-grained cake, and measure for measure is not as sweet as the granulated; if weighed there is not much if any difference. The receipts in this book are proportioned for patent flour; if pastry flour is used take about one-eighth more.

Never beat eggs until the last possible moment before using; in beating whites of eggs with a Dover beater, hold it as nearly as possible to the horizontal instead of perpendicular and there will be nearly one-half greater bulk of foam than when beaten as usual. Eggs will beat up lighter if laid on ice till chilled through before using. Baking powder should be sifted with a part of the flour and added with the white of egg at the last.

Measure exactly and use all the materials. A teaspoonful of butter left sticking to the measuring cup, a tablespoonful of milk spilled on the table, one-half an egg left not wiped from the shells or at the bottom of the bowl in which it was beaten, does make a difference in the cake. With a small palette knife it is possible to scrape out the last speck of butter, every atom of egg, each grain of sugar and flour.

In making butter cake mixtures observe the following order. Warm the bowl, and scald wooden spoon with boiling water, then wipe dry. Rub butter to a cream, add sugar and beat again until light. If the proportion of sugar is more than double the butter beat a part of it with the yolks of the eggs. Add a tablespoonful of flour before putting in any liquid to prevent curdling; beat in the beaten yolks, then add milk and flour alternately taking care not to let the mixture become very stiff nor very soft; lastly add the beaten whites and beat long and hard to make sure of having it smooth and fine grained. Fruit should be added last, or if in thin large pieces it may be put in layers as the dough is put into pans.

Cake is baked when it shrinks from the pan and stops hissing; or when a straw thrust into the center comes out clean. Let stand on a warm surface five minutes or less, then turn out onto a sieve or wire netting (a window screen will do), remove paper at once, peeling it back in narrow strips to avoid taking off the brown crust. If the cake should happen to burn, rasp the too brown portion with a coarse grater.

SPONGE CAKE, NO. 1.

Six eggs, once their weight in finest granulated sugar, one-half their weight in flour, one-half teaspoonful salt, the grated rind and juice of one lemon. Beat the eggs, yolks and whites together, with a spoon-whisk for twenty minutes, beating with a long, steady stroke; sift in the sugar with the left hand, keeping up the beating with the right, then add lemon juice and rind and lastly fold in the flour, not beating any more. If it has been put together right it will have a light spongy texture and seem rather dry. Bake in a rather deep tin about fifty minutes. Do not open the oven door for the first fifteen minutes, at the end of that time it should begin to rise, at the end of the next fifteen minutes it should double its bulk and by the end of the next twenty minutes it should be sufficiently browned and baked through.

SPONGE CAKE, NO. 2.

Three eggs beaten to a cream, one and one-half cups of sugar, add one-half cup of cold water, two cups of flour in which has been sifted two teaspoonfuls Star Crystal Baking Powder, one saltspoonful salt and flavoring to suit the taste. (N. B. Try grated rind of one-half lemon.) Beat hard for two minutes and bake thirty to forty minutes in a rather quick oven.

BERWICK SPONGE.

Same receipt as above but the cake is beaten five minutes for each ingredient added.

JELLY ROLL.

One cup flour, one cup sugar, one and one-half teaspoonfuls Star Crystal Baking Powder, three eggs well beaten. Mix in order given, beat well and pour into a smooth, well-greased pan; bake slow, spread jelly over and roll it up.

NOTE.—Have ready a smooth sheet of brown paper well dusted with powdered sugar, turn your cake onto it and spread quickly with the jelly which should be well broken with a fork if at all stiff. With a sharp knife trim off all the crusty edges and roll it by lifting one side of the paper. The cake will break if allowed to cool before rolling. To keep the roll perfectly round hang it up in a cloth. (Ed.) S.

CHILDREN'S SPONGE CAKE.

One and one-half cups flour, two teaspoonfuls Star Crystal Baking Powder, one cup sugar, two eggs broken into a cup and the cup filled with milk or cream. Stir all together in a mixing bowl, beat hard for five minutes and bake about ten minutes in muffin pans or a large pan with a chimney.

GRAHAM SPONGE CAKE.

Use receipts either No. 1 or 2, substituting sifted graham meal for flour and making the measure round instead of level.

SUNSHINE CAKE.

Eleven whites of eggs, six yolks of eggs, one teaspoonful cream of tartar, one and one-half cups sifted granulated sugar, one cup patent flour, one teaspoonful extract orange. Beat whites till stiff and flaky, then whisk in one-half the sugar, beat yolks very light and add flavor and one-half the sugar, put yolks and whites together and fold in flour and cream of tartar, mixing as quick as possible. Bake fifty to sixty minutes in a slow oven, using Angel Cake pan.

ANGEL CAKE, NO. 1.

One and one-half cups granulated sugar, measured after sifting, one cup of pastry flour, one teaspoonful cream of tartar, sift together eight times, then sift flour and sugar together three times. Beat the whites of eleven eggs with a wire beater, until they are dry and flaky. Pour over one teaspoonful vanilla, fold in the mixture of flour and sugar. Get it into a moderate oven as quickly as possible and bake about one hour. The pan should have a chimney and little legs on top so that when turned over a current of air can pass under it. Do not grease the pan. Never try to take it out but stand upside down till it drops of itself.

Mrs. Lincoln.

ANGEL FOOD, NO. 2.

Sift one pound of flour, one-half pound of powdered sugar, two teaspoonfuls Star Crystal Baking Powder together through a fine sieve, beat the whites of six eggs to a stiff froth, add one-half cup of cream and mix very light. Bake in good hot oven, be careful to not open the oven until done. S.

MACAROONS.

One-half pound of sugar, whites of three eggs, beat the eggs light, then add the sugar and beat them very stiff. Blanch one-half pound of almonds and pound them; two teaspoonfuls of rose water, one tablespoonful of flour; mix well, drop on greased paper, if they run too much add more flour. S.

BUTTER SPONGE CAKES.

MOUNTAIN SPONGE CAKE.

Beat four eggs, one cup of butter, one cup of sugar, to a light cream, then sift one quart of flour, three heaping teaspoonfuls of Star Crystal Baking Powder into the mixture, and milk enough to make the dough drop off the spoon; put in a well-buttered and papered pan and bake in a good hot oven. S.

CREAM SPONGE CAKE.

One quart of flour, one cup of butter, one pint of cream, three eggs, one cup of powdered sugar, two heaping teaspoonfuls of Star Crystal Baking Powder, rub butter into the sugar, then beat the yolks of the eggs and cream well together, stir into the flour, beat the whites of the eggs to a stiff froth, mix light; flavor and bake about thirty minutes. S.

SPONGE CAKE.

One and one-half quarts of flour, two heaping teaspoonfuls Star Crystal Baking Powder, the yolks of three eggs, one cup of sugar. Beat well with one-half cup of butter, the whites of the eggs beaten to a stiff froth, mix together with one and one-half cups of milk and bake in a hot oven. S.

ORANGE CAKE, NO. 1.

Two cups of flour, one-half cup of butter, the whites of five eggs, one cup of white sugar, one-half cup of cold water, two heaping teaspoonfuls Star Crystal Baking Powder, the juice and rind of one orange, bake like jelly cake and frost each layer.

S.

ORANGE CAKE, NO. 2.

Two eggs, one cup of sugar, one tablespoonful melted butter, one-half cup of milk, one and one-half cups of flour, two teaspoonfuls Star Crystal Baking Powder, one tablespoonful of orange juice, one teaspoonful grated rind, mix in order given; bake in square pan, split and fill with orange cream.

ORANGE CREAM.—Put into a cup the rind of one-half and the juice of one orange, one tablespoonful of lemon juice, and fill with hot water. Strain and put on to boil, add one tablespoonful corn starch wet with cold water and cook ten minutes, being careful not to scorch. Beat yolk of one egg with two heaping tablespoonfuls sugar, add to the mixture with one teaspoonful butter, let cook until the butter is dissolved, and cool. Fill the cake with cream and frost with orange icing.

BOSTON COOK BOOK.

LEMON CAKE.

Is made by the above receipt, using grated lemon peel instead of orange.

PINEAPPLE CAKE.

Same receipt using pineapple juice and pulp instead of orange, and frosting the top and sides with five-minute frosting given below.

ICE CREAM CAKE.

Make a sponge cake by No. 2, bake in three deep jelly tins and cool thoroughly; beat one pint thick sweet cream with sugar enough to sweeten to taste, flavor with vanilla; blanch and chop fine one pound almonds, stir into the cream and spread thick between the layers and on top.

ASHLAND CAKE.

One-half cup of butter, one-half cup of sweet milk, one cup flour, one cup sugar, one-half cup corn starch, whites of four eggs, one teaspoonful Star Crystal Baking Powder, ten drops extract lemon. Bake in two deep jelly tins.

FILLING FOR ABOVE.—Two cups granulated sugar, one-quarter cup of boiling water. Boil till it will spin then pour slowly boiling hot on to the well-beaten whites of two eggs beating all the time. Beat till thick enough not to run, then add one-half teaspoonful citric acid (powdered) one teaspoonful each of lemon and vanilla, spread between the layers and over the cake.

FIG LAYER CAKE.

One pound of flour, three eggs, three teaspoonfuls Star Crystal Baking Powder, three ounces of butter, one cup of sugar, mix well and bake in a hot oven; then chop one pound of figs, one-half pound of raisins very fine, beat the whites of two eggs and one-half cup of powdered sugar to a stiff froth, spread the figs on top of each layer and cover with frosting, put in the oven again for five minutes. S.

COCOANUT CAKE.

Four cups of flour, one cup of milk, three of sugar, five eggs beaten separately, save the whites of three eggs for icing; one cup of butter, three teaspoonfuls of Star Crystal Baking Powder, the half of a grated cocoanut and put into the mixture, the other half put with the whites of three eggs and one-half cup of powdered sugar, with a little orange water or lemon juice for icing. Bake the cakes in jelly tins, when done spread the icing between and on top and put in the oven for a few minutes. S.

FIG CAKE.

Two cups of sugar, one cup of butter, one of cold water with a teaspoonful of soda dissolved in it, three cups of raisins chopped fine, cinnamon and nutmegs, four eggs, one pound of figs, use the figs split in halves, covering them well with the cake to prevent burning. Bake in layers, frosting between each layer; make as stiff as pound cake, cut with a very sharp knife to prevent crumbling. This receipt will make two cakes. S.

WASHINGTON PIE.

Two cups of powdered sugar, one cup of butter, one quart of flour, three teaspoonfuls Star Crystal Baking Powder, one cup of milk, two eggs; mix well, rub butter and sugar into the eggs, mix well together. Bake in jelly tins, pour whipped cream between the layers and serve and cut like pie.　　　　S.

WASHINGTON PIE, NO. 2.

Make sponge cake No. 2, baking it in jelly cake tins, spread with whipped cream or jam and pile whipped cream on top.

ALMOND CHOCOLATE CAKE.

Three cups of flour, one of sugar, one-half cup of butter, four eggs, rub butter and sugar to a cream, then add eggs, flour, three teaspoonfuls Star Crystal Baking Powder, mix thoroughly and add milk last into the mixture; pour in a square, well-buttered pan and bake thirty minutes. When cold spread chocolate frosting on top and ornament with almonds.　　　　S.

QUEEN CHOCOLATE CAKE.

One pound of flour, two heaping teaspoonfuls Star Crystal Baking Powder; beat three eggs, one cup of milk with one-half cup of melted butter, add the flour, flavor with lemon, mix thoroughly and bake in hot oven. When cold make a chocolate frosting and ornament with walnuts.　　　　S.

SNOW FLAKE CAKE.

Two cups flour, three eggs, one-half cup of sugar, one-half cup of butter, three-quarter cup of milk, two heaping teaspoonfuls Star Crystal Baking Powder, the whites of two eggs and one-half cup of sugar beaten to a froth; mix well, pour in tins, bake like layer cakes and frost each layer and sprinkle with cocoanut.　　　　S.

ONE EGG CAKE.

Two cups of flour, one cup of sweet milk, one cup of sugar, the size of an egg melted butter, one egg, three teaspoonfuls Star Crystal Baking Powder, mix well and bake in a hot oven.　　　　S.

CHRISTMAS EVE CAKE.

One pound of flour, six eggs, three teaspoonfuls Star Crystal Baking Powder, one cup of best butter, two cups of powdered sugar, beat the whites of the eggs to a very stiff froth, stir well with a cup of cream beaten with the yolks of the eggs and flavor with arrack or rum, mix light and bake slowly in not too hot an oven. When cold make plain icing and pour over. S.

STAR CRYSTAL CAKE.

One and one-half pounds powdered sugar, one-half pound of butter, yolks of four eggs, one pound of flour, two heaping teaspoonfuls Star Crystal Baking Powder, sift well, rub eggs and sugar into the butter, beat the whites of the eggs to a stiff froth, flavor and mix light, then bake in hot oven on layer tins, when cold spread icing and grated cocoanut between the layers and on top. S.

DROP CAKES.

One quart of flour, three teaspoonfuls Star Crystal Baking Powder, sift well, one cup butter, three eggs, one cup of sugar, rub butter and sugar into the eggs and add milk enough to make a light dough, then drop with a spoon into little forms and bake in hot oven. S.

ALMOND CAKE.

One cup of milk, one cup of sugar, one-half cup butter, two and one-half cups of flour, four eggs, add two heaping teaspoonfuls of Star Crystal Baking Powder to the flour and sift twice then set aside. Beat butter and sugar to a light cream, pound one cup of almonds add milk, then the eggs beaten seperately into which stir the flour lightly and bake in hot oven. S.

WEDDING CAKE.

One pound of flour, one pound of powdered sugar, one dozen eggs, one-half pound of butter, beat eggs and sugar together over a very slow fire until it thickens, cool off but keep on stirring, then add flour and melted butter into the mixture and put in the flour last, paper your pan and bake about forty minutes. S.

CLEVELAND CAKE.

Sift one-half pound of corn starch, one-half pound of wheat flour, one pound powdered sugar, three heaping teaspoonfuls Star Crystal Baking Powder into six eggs, a pint of sweet milk, mix thoroughly and pour one-half cup of melted butter into the mixture, put in a square baking pan and bake slow.　　　　S.

FRENCH LOAF.

Three cups of flour, three eggs, three teaspoonfuls Star Crystal Baking Powder, two cups of powdered sugar, one cup of butter, mix well, beat the whites of the three eggs to a stiff froth, rub butter and sugar to a light cream, add one cup of milk, beat the yolks of the eggs well and flavor to taste, mix again, then pour the mixture into a well-papered and buttered pan, sprinkle a little powdered sugar over the cake before baking. It is well to cover it when first putting in the oven in order not to harden the top too soon.　　　　S.

EASTER SUNDAY CAKE.

Two pounds of flour, one of sugar, one cup of raisins, three heaping teaspoonfuls Star Crystal Baking Powder, three eggs beaten separately, the whites of the eggs to a stiff froth, beat the yolks of the eggs into a pint of milk, mix well together and be careful in mixing the froth into the mixture last, paper and butter your pans well, and bake in loaf. This will give three cakes.　　　　S.

BEAUMONT CAKE.

One pound of powdered sugar, one-half pound butter, yolks of six eggs, one quart flour, three heaping teaspoonfuls Star Crystal Baking Powder, one cup of raisins, a wine glass of arrack, then beat the whites of six eggs to a stiff froth, mix all together well and bake in loaf; when cold spread plain icing on top.　S.

MARBLE CAKE.

WHITE PART.—Whites of four eggs, one cup of white sugar, one-half cup of butter, one-half cup sweet milk, two heaping teaspoonfuls Star Crystal Baking Powder, one teaspoonful of vanilla or lemon, and two and a half cups of sifted flour.

BLACK PART.—The yolks of four eggs, one cup of brown sugar, one-half cup of molasses, one-half cup of butter, one-half cup of sour milk, one teaspoonful of cloves, one of cinnamon, one teaspoonful of mace, one nutmeg, one-half teaspoonful soda, and one and one-half cups of sifted flour; put it in the cake dish alternately, first one part and then the other. The pan should be lined with buttered paper. S.

GOLD AND SILVER CAKE.

One-half cup butter, one and one-half cups sugar, two cups flour, four eggs, one teaspoonful Star Crystal Baking Powder, one-half cup milk. Use the whites for one cake, the yolks for the other. Flavor the white with extract almond, the yellow with lemon. Frost with white and yellow frosting.

COMPOSITION CAKE.

Five cups flour, three cups sugar, two cups butter, one cup of milk, two teaspoonfuls Star Crystal Baking Powder, one wine glass of wine, five eggs, one nutmeg; add one pound of raisins (if you want the cake rich.) Beat the sugar and butter to a cream, beat the whites of above five eggs to a stiff froth, beat wine and spice into flour well; mix together light and bake one hour. S.

CREAM FRUIT CAKE.

One quart flour, one cup of butter, one and one-half cups sugar, three teaspoonfuls Star Crystal Baking Powder, four eggs, chop one-half pound of raisins, one-half pound almonds, one-quarter pound citron, very fine. Beat the whites of the eggs to a stiff froth, mix well, add cream enough to make the dough light, butter and paper your pan and bake in good hot oven.

S.

BIRTHDAY CAKE.

One pound of butter, one pound of sugar, nine eggs, one pound flour, three pounds currants, two pounds stoned raisins, one-half tea cup wine or brandy, from one-half to three-quarters pounds citron, one grated nutmeg, a little mace and cinnamon. Rub the butter and sugar together, when light add first the yolks and then the whites of the eggs, the yolks and whites of eggs to be beaten separately, then put in nearly all your flour, keeping out just enough to dust your raisins, and separate them; cut your citron in such slices as you like and put in as you put the cake in the pan; after mixing your fruit in the cake, grease a four-quart pan carefully, line with brown paper, lightly buttered. Put the cake in and bake in not too hot an oven. When baked take it out of the pan, paper and all, and let cool. The next day, to keep it moist, put it back in the pan and keep it tightly covered. S.

FRUIT CAKE.

One pound of butter, one of sugar, one of flour, twelve eggs, one-half gill of brandy, one nutmeg, one-half teaspoonful of cloves, two teaspoonfuls cinnamon, one and one-half pounds of raisins, one and one-half pounds of currants, one pound of citron. Seed the raisins and chop them quite fine; wash the citron in hot water, wipe it dry and slice it in small pieces; beat butter and sugar to a cream, add the flour with the brandy and the spices, and last the fruit. Mix the whole well together, paper your pan and bake in not too hot an oven about four hours.
S.

SCOTCH PLUM CAKE.

One-quarter peck of flour, one pound of sugar, three pounds currants, one pound of chopped raisins, one-quarter ounce of mace and cloves, a grated nutmeg, peel of lemon cut fine, one-half pound of blanched almonds beaten with rose water, mix well, then melt two pounds of butter in a pint of cream, put in a glass of sherry, one of brandy, twelve eggs, the yolks and whites beaten apart, and one-half pint of good yeast; strain this into the dry ingredients, beat a full hour, butter your hoop, throw in plenty chips of citron, lemon and orange candy, as you put in your batter, and bake in a good hot oven. S.

OLD-FASHIONED CUP CAKE.

One cup of butter, one-half cup of milk, one and one-half cups sugar, three cups flour, three eggs beaten separately, two teaspoonfuls Star Crystal Baking powder, one saltspoonful mace, one-half teaspoonful extract lemon. Cream the butter and add sugar gradually, then the yolks of eggs, then the flavoring; sift the baking powder with the flour and add alternately with the milk, lastly beat in the whites. This is the foundation for almost all the butter cakes given previously. Use one-half the butter and scant the flour and it makes all the layer cake mixtures. Color one-third the dough with spices and add one-half cup currants and chopped raisins, bake in jelly cake tins, placing the dark layer between the two white ones, fasten together with frosting and cover top and sides thickly with boiled frosting. Omit the milk and use six eggs and it is a rich loaf cake, etc. MRS. CAMPBELL.

POUND CAKE.

One pound sugar, one pound butter, ten eggs, one pound flour, one saltspoonful each salt, mace and nutmeg. Bake in two narrow loaves about one hour.

WEDDING CAKE.

To the above mixture add two eggs, making twelve in all, two teaspoonfuls each of cinnamon and mace, one teaspoonful each of nutmeg and allspice, one-half teaspoonful cloves, one ounce chocolate dissolved over warm water, three pounds raisins (weighed after seeding), three pounds Sultana raisins, three pounds currants, one and one-half pounds citron, two ounces each of candied lemon and orange peel, one pound shredded almonds which have been blanched and dried, two ounces brandy, two ounces port wine, two tablespoonfuls strained honey. Let the flour used for drying the fruit be in addition to the one pound of the batter. Mix well and rest a few hours, over night, if convenient; mix again before putting into pans.

ENGLISH WAFERS.

One and one-half pounds flour, one pound sugar, one pound of butter, one cup of milk, rub the butter, sugar and flour together, then add the milk, mix well, turn it out and work it until it becomes perfectly smooth. Roll into sheets, cut with small cutter, then place on tins and bake in not too hot an oven. It will take a few minutes to knead all the ingredients into a dough, but as the quantity of milk is quite sufficient it would spoil them to add more. S.

NEW YEAR CAKES.

One pound of butter, one and one-half pounds of sugar, three pounds of flour, two tablespoonfuls of caraway seed, one-half teaspoonful of soda dissolved in a cupful of milk, cut long and print, or cut as cookies. S.

GINGER SNAPS, NO. 1.

Work one-half pound of butter into one and one-half pounds of good flour, mix it with one-half pound of molasses, one-quarter pound of brown sugar, a teaspoonful of ginger and the same of caraway seeds; mix well together and form it into cakes not larger than a crown piece, place in a baking pan and bake in a moderate oven. S.

GINGER SNAPS, NO. 2.

One cup molasses, one teaspoonful soda, one-half cup sugar, one-half cup butter, one tablespoonful ginger, flour to roll very thin. Mix molasses, sugar, ginger and butter, stir over the fire until the butter is melted, then stir in quickly four cups of flour in which has been sifted the pulverized soda. Knead the dough with more flour until stiff enough to roll out easily. Roll as thin as pasteboard and bake in a quick oven.

SOFT MOLASSES COOKIES.

One cup molasses, two tablespoonfuls warm milk or water, one tablespoonful ginger, one-half cup of soft butter, one teaspoonful soda, flour to mix soft as can be handled on the board. Mix in order given, dissolving soda in the milk. Shape on a floured board into balls the size of a hickory nut. Lay on a sheet and flatten to one-half inch thick.—*School Kitchen Text-Book.*

WATER GINGERBREAD.

Two cups molasses, one cup warm water, one-half cup each of butter and lard, (heaping), one teaspoonful soda, one tablespoonful ginger, flour to knead soft. Mix in order given, roll out about one inch thick on baking sheets and bake about one-half hour in moderate oven. It should be crisp when new.

SPICE GINGERBREAD.

One quart flour, an egg of butter rubbed in, one teaspoonful Star Crystal Baking Powder, one teaspoonful *fine* soda, mixed in dry, one teaspoonful each of cinnamon, cloves, mace and salt, two cups molasses, one cup boiling water. Beat hard; bake in a loaf very slowly.

BEDFORD JUMBLES.

Two cups sugar, one cup butter, beaten well together; add one-half cup flour and four well-beaten eggs, one tablespoonful vanilla and flour enough to roll out. One-half cup grated cocoanut is a delicious addition, or cover them with finely shred almonds.

PLAIN COOKIES.

Use above rule, adding two teaspoonfuls Star Crystal Baking Powder to the flour, and one-half cup of milk to the dough, and two teaspoonfuls caraway seeds. Bake quickly.

HERMITS.

Add one-half cup stoned and chopped raisins to the receipt for Bedford Jumbles and bake one-quarter inch thick.

PFEFFER NUSS.

Four pounds flour, twenty-five ounces almonds, four ounces bitter almonds, one teaspoonful cinnamon, rind and juice of one lemon, two and one-half pounds strained honey, boiled with two pounds sugar and poured boiling hot on the flour, one ounce (cooking) potash dissolved in wine glass of water. Knead till perfectly smooth, shape in nuts and bake in moderate oven until dry through.

SNOWFLAKES.

Five eggs, one-half pound of flour, one-quarter pound of butter, one cup of powdered sugar, two teaspoonfuls Star Crystal Baking Powder; cream the butter and work the eggs into it. Sift flour, sugar and baking powder together, adding a little milk if necessary to thin, cut out with a cutter and fry in hot lard.

ADDITIONAL RECIPES.

ADDITIONAL RECIPES.

ADDITIONAL RECIPES.

FROSTING.

FIVE MINUTE FROSTING.

The white of one egg, one teaspoonful lemon juice, one scant cup of powdered sugar stirred together until the sugar is all wet, then beat with a fork for just five minutes; spread quickly on the cake while warm.—*Boston Cook Book.*

BOILED FROSTING.

Boil one cup granulated sugar, a speck of cream tartar, and one-third cup of water until it spins a thread when dropped from the spoon, then pour in a fine stream onto the white of an egg beaten stiff, beating as you pour, continue beating until stiff enough to stand alone, add flavoring and spread on the cake with a knife dipped in warm water.

ORNAMENTAL FROSTING.

One cup sifted powdered sugar, one teaspoonful lemon juice, the white of one egg; beat the egg until it is all frothy but not dry, then sprinkle over three teaspoonfuls sugar and beat five minutes; add one teaspoonful each five minutes till quite thick, then put in the lemon juice. Beat with a fork and when a point of it will stand in any position it is ready to press through a pastry tube onto the cake, which should be already covered with a smooth plain frosting.

GOLDEN FROSTING.

Beat two yolks of egg with one cup sugar and one-half teaspoonful old Jamaica rum, add more sugar if not stiff enough to hold its place.

CHOCOLATE FROSTING.

Melt one ounce chocolate, add one teaspoonful powdered sugar, and add to the boiled frosting till it is dark as you wish.

ORANGE FROSTING.

Grate the thin rind of an orange and soak it one-half hour in three teaspoonfuls lemon juice. Squeeze the juice through a fine muslin and use like the lemon in five-minute frosting.

FROSTING FOR CAKES.

Ten teaspoonfuls powdered sugar to the white of an egg, beat five minutes for each spoonful of sugar.

PLAIN ICING.

One cup powdered sugar, one tablespoonful lemon juice, about one tablespoonful boiling water; beat hard till smooth and semi-transparent. Spread on the cake as soon as taken from the oven.

CHOCOLATE ICING.

Omit the lemon juice from the above recipe and add three heaping tablespoonfuls of pulverized chocolate.

ADDITIONAL RECIPES.

ADDITIONAL RECIPES.

PASTRY.

Don't make it! But if it must be made, this is the way to do it:

One pound flour (one quart), one teaspoonful salt, one-third pound butter, well rubbed together till like meal. If your hands are hot, chop it together without touching it with the hands. Mix stiff as possible with ice water and pat out on the board to about one-third of an inch thick; lay this sheet of paste on ice while two-thirds pound butter is washed and worked in cold water until waxy. Divide it in four parts and pat each out to as thin a cake as you can, it is no matter if it is broken through in holes. Set these sheets of butter on ice also. Now dust the board and pin slightly with flour, place the sheet of paste on it and one sheet of butter on the middle of the paste; fold the paste over the butter in such a way as to divide the paste in thirds, then turn over the ends letting them meet in the middle; the paste is now in rectangular shape and with a little care in rolling can be kept so through all the subsequent foldings and rollings. Roll out to one-quarter inch thick and fold as before, but without butter. The third time of folding enclose the second piece of butter, and continue adding it at every alternate rolling until it has all been used; as there were four sheets of butter that will make eight times folding and rolling the paste. Finally give one, two or three extra turns, as your patience holds out; lay on ice until needed for use; it is better to lie for several hours before being baked. If the paste sticks to the board or pin lay on ice until chilled through, scrape the board clean, polish with a dry cloth and dust with fresh flour before trying again. A stone slab is a comfort but not at all necessary. Use as little flour in rolling as possible, but use enough to keep the paste dry. Roll with a light, even, long stroke in every direction, but never work the rolling-pin back and forth, as that kneads the paste and toughens it, besides breaking the bubbles of air. The number of layers of butter and paste makes it flaky, but every bubble of air that is folded in helps it to rise and puff in baking.

TO BAKE PUFF PASTE.

The dough should be ice cold when put into the oven. If it softens while being cut into the desired shape, place it on the ice again until hard. The oven should be as hot as for baking white bread; set it on the floor of the oven at first until risen to its full height, then slip a grate under to keep from burning while baking through and browning; if the oven is too hot the paste will set and scorch before it is risen; if too cool it will melt and spread or slip out of shape. The exact temperature can only be acquired by practice.

Patty shells should rise in ten minutes and then take about twenty minutes longer to bake through and brown. There will usually be a little soft dough in the center that should be picked out with a fork, taking great care not to break through the side or bottom crust. To shape the paste for patties, etc., roll to about one-third inch in thickness and stamp out with a two and one-quarter inch cutter twice as many pieces as you wish shells. Cut centers from one-half of them, leaving the rim about one-half inch wide. Lay these rings on the whole rounds, pressing them down that they may stick together. In very cold weather it may be needful to wet the top of the large rounds near the edge to make sure that the rings shall not slip. To make very deep shells roll the paste about one-eighth inch thick and lay on *two* rings, or even *three*, but they are troublesome to bake as they are apt to slip to one side.

TARTS.

Are rolled as thin as convenient and cut with a fluted cutter. They are served cold, filled with jelly or jam.

BOUCHEES.

Are made small, about one and one-half inches in diameter and very deep; they are served hot, filled with very highly seasoned meat or shell fish, dressed with mayonnaise or sauce tartare. The filling may be either hot or cold.

RISSOLES.

Can be made of the trimmings of puff paste rolled very thin, cut in three inch rounds. Put a teaspoonful of filling in the center, cover with another round, wet the edges with white of egg to ensure their being fastened, and fry a few seconds in very hot fat till a handsome color.

FOR PIES.

Roll the paste out about one-third of an inch thick, then roll up and cut from the end of the roll. Turn each piece on the side so that the folds show the rings, pat out flat, then rol a trifle larger than the plate. This should be used for the upper crust only, and for a rim if desired; if used for under crust it is always sodden and indigestible.

PLAIN PASTRY.

One cup of flour, heaping, one saltspoonful Star Crystal Baking Powder, one saltspoonful salt, one-quarter cup lard, one-quarter cup butter; mix baking powder and salt with the flour; rub in the lard and butter till fine and dry like meal. Mix to a stiff paste with ice water; this makes a tender, crispy crust, but not in the least flaky. If baked quickly and thoroughly it is as little hurtful to the digestion as any pastry can be. To make it somewhat flaky rub in only the lard, pat and roll out to one-third inch thick, dot on one-half the butter in thin pieces, dust with flour and fold in thirds; pat and roll out again, dot with remainder of butter and roll up like a jelly roll; cut from the end as directed for puff paste and it will give a fairly handsome crust if properly done. All pastry needs a quick oven at first to keep it from melting. *Never grease the pie plate.* All pies made with an upper crust should have holes cut to let the steam escape or the crust will be likely to be sodden on the under side. Tin or granite ware plates are much the best, as they cannot soak grease and bake the under crust more quickly and perfectly. The English fashion of baking all fruit pies in deep dishes, with no under crust, is admirable, being far more delicious as well as more wholesome. Their meat and game pies, made in the same way, win favor wherever they are introduced.

APPLE PIE.

Line a plate with plain paste, fill with apples that have been pared, cored and cut in eighths until it is piled as high above the edge as the bottom of the plate is below. Cover with either plain or puff paste and bake till apples are soft, about thirty minutes. (Try them with a fork.) When done boil three-quarters cup sugar in one-quarter cup of water five minutes. Pour this syrup boiling hot through the holes in the crust. Tilt the pie a little until the syrup shows through on every side. If you choose to put in the sugar before baking, sprinkle three-quarters cup over the apples when the pie is little more than one-half full, cover with remainder of apples and put on crust as usual. Take a strip of cotton one inch wide and long enough to go around the plate, wring it out of cold water and bind the edge of the pie with it. If pulled from the pie as soon as taken from the oven, it will leave no mark.

PIE PLANT PIE.

Wash the stalks and cut into inch bits without peeling, pour boiling water over it and let it stand ten minutes, dredge lightly with flour; for a ten-inch plate allow a heaping cup of sugar, dot with one tablespoonful butter cut in bits the size of a pea, cover and bake in a very quick oven for the first ten minutes, then more slowly until done, about thirty minutes in all.

PUMPKIN PIE.

One cup of stewed and sifted pumpkin (or squash), one level teaspoonful salt, one saltspoonful mace, one teaspoonful cinnamon, two-thirds cup of sugar, one beaten egg well mixed together, pour over a cup each of cream and milk boiling hot, fill the plate and set into oven as quickly as possible; if pumpkin is watery add one teaspoonful flour. It is done when it rises well in the middle. A rim of puff paste can be laid around the edge of the plate if liked, if used it should be at least one inch wide and the edge that goes down into the squash rolled very thin.

CUSTARD PIE.

Line plate as for squash. Heat one pint of milk, rub one teaspoonful flour smooth with one-half cup cold milk, add to the boiling milk and cook five minutes. Pour on to three beaten eggs, one-half cup of sugar, one saltspoonful salt and flavor to taste, one-half teaspoonful lemon or one teaspoonful vanilla. Strain hot into a deep plate, bake slowly, never letting it boil. It is done when a knife blade makes a clean cut.

LEMON PIE, NO. 1.

One cup of milk, one cup of sugar, one tablespoonful cornstarch cooked over hot water for at least fifteen minutes, one saltspoonful salt, the yolks of three eggs and the white of one egg, grated rind and juice of one lemon. Fill the paste while hot and bake quick. Beat the whites of two eggs stiff, add slowly two tablespoonfuls of sifted powdered sugar, spread over the pie as soon as it comes out of the oven and return it to dry and brown slightly.

N. B. If oven is very hot leave the door ajar.

LEMON PIE, NO. 2.

Grated rind and juice of one lemon, one cup sugar, one-half cup of milk, two tablespoonfuls cracker dust, two eggs, one saltspoonful salt. Good baked in old fashioned way between two crusts.

LEMON PIE, NO. 3.

Mix three tablespoonfuls cornstarch, one saltspoonful salt, one and one-half cups sugar, stir into one pint boiling water and cook ten minutes. Then add grated rind and juice of two large lemons, the beaten yolks of four eggs, then the whites beaten stiff folded in lightly. Bake in two pies about twenty minutes in a rather quick oven. Meringue as in No. 1.

CHERRY TART.

Pick over one and one-half pounds of cherries; turn a tiny cup upside down in the middle of a deep pie dish, fill around it with the fruit, add moist sugar to taste. Lay a wide strip of plain paste around the edge of the dish, cover and press the edges firmly together with a pastry jagger, bake in hot oven and serve with powdered sugar sprinkled thickly on top. All juicy fruits are most excellent cooked in the same way.   S.

BOSTON CREAM PIE.

One pint of sweet milk, two eggs, three tablespoonfuls sifted flour, five tablespoonfuls of sugar, put two-thirds of the milk on to boil and stir the sugar and flour in what is left. When the rest boils put in the whole and stir until it cooks thoroughly. When cool flavor with lemon or vanilla. Bake with two crusts.

S.

POTATO PIE.

Boil six sweet potatoes, mash and sift them through a coarse sieve, add three pints of milk to a pint of pulp, a tablespoonful of melted butter, two eggs, a teacup of sugar, one-half a teaspoonful salt, nutmeg or lemon to flavor, and bake with an under crust of rich paste.

S.

APPLE TART.

Stew one dozen apples till quite soft, take out any hard pieces, beat them to a pulp, allow six ounces of sugar, five eggs, the grated rind of a lemon, five ounces of melted butter, line a dish with puff paste, pour in the mixture and bake at once.

S.

MINCE PIES, PLAIN.

Two coffee cups chopped beef and small piece, about 4 ounces, of fat salt pork, four coffee cups sugar, one nutmeg, one coffee cup molasses, two lemons, rind and juice, or sour orange, four teaspoonfuls salt, two cups cider, boiled with the molasses, four teaspoonfuls cinnamon, four cups of chopped fruit (raisins, citron, currants), one teaspoonful cloves, one cup suet, finely chopped. Mix and scald, pack down in jars and pour a little brandy on top. When used, add six cups apple and stoned raisins ad lib.

MINCE PIES, RICHER.

One pound fresh beef, one pound tongue, one-half pound salt pork (scalded) chopped very fine, one pound large raisins, seeded, one pound Sultana raisins, one pound currants, three-quarter pound "A" sugar, three-quarter granulated sugar caramel, one pint of rich stock, one pint of boiled cider, fruit juice or soft jelly, simmer till well blended. Add one tablespoonful salt, two teaspoonfuls cinnamon, one teaspoonful allspice, one teaspoonful cloves, one teaspoonful mace, one teaspoonful nutmeg, one-half pound citron, shredded. Cool and taste; add more seasoning if liked. Pack in glass jars, pouring two tablespoonfuls of brandy on the top of each. When ready to use, add two and one-half cups of chopped raw apples to each cup of the mince; partly cook and put into the pies hot, adding lemon (grated rind and juice) and rose water, if liked.

EGG MINCE MEAT.

Chop six hard boiled eggs very fine, double the quantity of beef suet, one pound of currants, mince the peel of two lemons, six tablespoonfuls of sweet wine, a little mace, nutmeg and salt to taste, add one-quarter of a pound candied orange and citron, cut into thin slices, mix well together and press it into a jar until needed. Add apple as for pies made with meat.   S.

BRAMBLES.

One lemon grated whole, one cup raisins, seeded and chopped fine, one-half cup sugar, one egg, one tablespoonful cracker dust, bake in "turnovers" or patty pans or better still, roll trimmings of puff paste as thin as possible, put a layer on a baking sheet, spread with above mixture and cover with another flat of paste. Mark off with a pastry jagger in strips four inch long by two inch wide and bake in a quick oven. These are nice with a thin icing and are delicious with cocoa for lunch. Another, richer filling is made by chopping very fine one-quarter pound figs, two ounces citron, one-quarter cup pistachio nuts (or almonds), two ounces seeded raisins, add one egg well beaten and use like the above.

CHEESE STRAWS.

Equal measures of flour and grated cheese, the richer the cheese the better. To each cupful allow one saucespoonful salt and a speck of cayenne. Mix to a stiff paste with ice water, roll to one-eighth inch and mark off in straws before baking.

ADDITIONAL RECIPES.

ADDITIONAL RECIPES.

ADDITIONAL RECIPES.

Puddings and Other Desserts.

ENGLISH OR CHRISTMAS PLUM PUDDING.

One and one-half pounds bread crumbs, two ounces citron, one-half pound flour, two ounces almonds, blanched and shredded, two pounds suet, chopped fine, two small nutmegs, grated, two pounds currants, one lemon, juice and grated rind, two pounds sugar, one teaspoonful salt, two ounces candied lemon peel, sixteen eggs, one wine glass of brandy, and enough milk to make a stiff paste. Mix in order given and boil for eight hours in a buttered mold or floured pudding cloth. The water must not stop boiling. When it is to be used, plunge into boiling water and cook for two hours more. Stick a sprig of holly in the top, pour two tablespoonfuls brandy over and bring to the table blazing. Serve with English sauce.

ANOTHER.

One-half pound chopped suet, one scant cup of brown sugar, one-quarter pound currants, one-half cup of brandy, one-half pound raisins, one-half cup of milk, one-half pound flour, one tablespoonful mixed spice, one ounce each of candied lemon and orange, one ounce citron, one saltspoonful salt, three eggs, rind of one lemon grated. Mix well, let rest two hours or more, pour into a buttered and floured cloth (or mold), boil forty-eight hours. Miss Hammond.

ENGLISH SAUCE.

Three yolks eggs, two lumps sugar well rubbed on lemon rind, one-half cup sugar, one-half saucespoonful salt, one-quarter cup sherry. Add one cup of milk, set in hot water and heat till light and frothy.

ANY DAY PLUM PUDDING.

One cup of chopped suet, one cup of raisins, one cup of currants, one-half cup of citron, one egg, one cup of sweet milk, three and one-half cups of flour, one teaspoonful salt, one teaspoonful Star Crystal Baking Powder; put into a bag and boil three hours.   S.

SPICE PUDDING.

One cup of milk, one cup flour, heaping, one cup molasses, one cup cornmeal, one-half teaspoonful allspice, one-half cup chopped suet or broken butter, one teaspoonful salt, one teaspoonful soda, one-half teaspoonful cloves, one teaspoonful cinnamon, one cup raisins or chopped figs or dates or sweet apples. Steam three hours in a mold with a chimney.

POOR MAN'S PUDDING.

One cup rice, well picked and washed, one-half cup sugar, two quarts milk, one teaspoonful salt, one-half teaspoonful cinnamon; bake very slowly for three to four hours, keeping covered as much as possible until the last fifteen minutes, then lift the cover to brown the top. It should be creamy and not dry when done.

TAPIOCA PUDDING.

Two ounces tapioca, boiled in one-half pint of water until it begins to melt, than add one-half pint of milk and boil until the tapioca becomes very thick, add a very well beaten egg, sugar and flavor to taste and bake one hour.   S.

ORANGE PUDDING.

Four oranges peeled and picked to pieces and put into a pudding dish with two cups of sugar, put a quart of milk, yolks of three eggs, and two teaspoonfuls of corn starch on to boil. Take off, cool it and pour over the oranges, beat the whites of the eggs to a stiff froth, put over the pudding and bake to light brown.   S.

RICE WITH PEARS.

Boil one and one-half cups of rice into a pint of milk, when tender put in a pinch of cinnamon and nutmeg and let it get real cool; beat three eggs, and mix then with the rice, butter a mold, put the rice into a bag and let boil for one-half hour, turn it out, lay around the baked pears, garnish with slices of lemon.

S.

STEAMED APPLES.

Fill a pie plate with tart juicy apples, quartered and cored, cover with baking powder crust, (one cup flour, one-half cup of butter, two teaspoonfuls of Star Crystal Baking Powder well mixed,) steam or cook on top of stove until the apples are tender, then set in oven to brown the crust, serve with any sauce preferred. S.

COMPOTE OF FRUIT.

One pound flour, one cup sugar, two eggs, two tablespoonfuls butter, three teaspoonfuls Star Crystal Baking Powder, one cup of milk, mix well and pour into a dripping pan and bake ten minutes. When done spread any kind of fruit on top. Pour a light custard over and bake again for ten minutes. S.

POOR MAN'S FRITTERS.

Cut a stale cake into slices of one and one-half inches in thickness, pour over them a little good cream and fry lightly in fresh butter. When done place fruit on each slice. S.

CAKE FRITTERS.

Take stale cake, cut into square pieces, soak them in a little sweet cider, then make a batter of one cup of flour, one of milk, two eggs, one teaspoonful of Star Crystal Baking Powder, dip the pieces into the batter and fry in hot lard. S.

GERMAN PUFF.

One pint milk, one pound flour, three tablespoonfuls butter, four eggs, beat the yolks until thick, warm the milk to which add the butter, when cool stir in the yolks, put the flour in a pan and stir in the above, whisk the whites and stir through very lightly, butter a long square pan which fill half with the mixture and bake in hot oven. Serve hot with any sauce preferred. S.

ADDITIONAL RECIPES.

PUDDING SAUCES.

APRICOT SAUCE.

Put four ounces of Apricot marmalade into a sauce pan with one ounce of fresh butter and one-half cupful of water; set over fire and stir with a wooden spoon until it begins to boil, then take from the fire, add one-half cup full of Kirsch (or brandy), let boil up once and serve with apricot or apple dumplings.

CHOCOLATE SAUCE.

One pint of milk, one tablespoonful of corn starch, a speck of salt, one-half cup of sugar cooked together for twenty minutes, stirring very often. Scrape two ounces of chocolate and melt over hot water, then stir into the boiling milk.

Beat the whites of two eggs stiff, and add gradually one-half cupful of powdered sugar, then the unbeaten yolks and stir all into the boiling mixture. Cook one minute longer, add one teaspoonful of vanilla extract and serve either hot or cold. It is especially nice with corn starch, rice or bread puddings.

CREAMY SAUCE.

One heaping teaspoonful butter, softened, two cups powdered sugar, one well-beaten egg rubbed to a cream together, add one-half cup thick cream and one teaspoonful vanilla. If it should seperate set it over hot water and stir until smooth again, keep on ice till wanted.

ENGLISH ORANGE SAUCE.

Put in a sauce pan four egg yolks with four ounces of powdered sugar, and stir with a wooden spoon until it becomes of a whitish color. Add one cupful of sweet cream, little by little, beating continually, then grate in the rind of an orange. Place the pan on a slow fire and stir well for four minutes, being careful not to let it boil; take it off; strain through a sieve over the pudding and serve very hot.

CARAMEL SAUCE.

Brown sugar in a clean frying pan until a light coffee color, add an equal measure of water and simmer until the sugar dissolves. Good either hot or cold.

FIG PUDDING SAUCE.

Four large figs cut into bits and simmered in water enough to cover until very soft, rub through a fine sieve, add enough water to make one pint in all, add one cup sugar, three level teaspoonfuls cornstarch and boil ten minutes, then one teaspoonful cornstarch and boil ten minutes, then one teaspoonful butter, the juice of one-half lemon (one tablespoonful) and serve as soon as the butter is melted.

GERMAN SAUCE.

One cup sugar, one-half cup water boiled fifteen minutes, beat the yolks of three eggs, and add the syrup. Set over hot water and beat with a whisk until it begins to thicken, then add one tablespoonful butter, three tablespoonfuls brandy and the whites of three eggs beaten dry. Stir a few minutes to cook the eggs and serve with any plum pudding.

ENGLISH SAUCE. (*See page 57.*)

ICED MADEIRA SAUCE.

Boil together one cupful of sugar and one cupful of water for fifteen minutes, than pour half of it into a small pail with the juice of one large orange, two tablespoonfuls of lemon juice and one-half cupful of Sicily Madeira. Set this into a freezing mixture and stir occasionally. Let the remaining half of the syrup boil five minutes more, then beat it slowly into the beaten whites of two eggs. Beating till they begin to stiffen; set away to cool until the frozen mixture is as stiff as can be stirred easily.

Beat in the meringue and it is ready to use, but will not hurt to stand for some time. A most delicious sauce for any frozen or ice-cold pudding.

WHIPPED CREAM.

Plain whipped cream, sweetened and flavored according to the dish on which it is to be served, makes an excellent sauce for many desserts; it is elegant and good enough for almost any pudding. To make a light whip a whip churn should always be used. A Dover beater or fork will whip the cream but it will always be solid rather than light and there is danger of bringing the cream to butter.

SYRUP SAUCES.

Boil two cups sugar with two tablespoonfuls water till it thickens slightly, take from the fire, stir in one teaspoonful butter and either lemon or orange juice or any fruit syrup, wine, brandy, cordial or any flavoring extract as preferred.

PLAIN SAUCE.

Two cups water, one cup sugar, boiling; stir in one tablespoonful cornstarch, wet with cold water, one lump sugar well rubbed on lemon rind, one teaspoonful butter and any flavoring preferred as in receipt above. Care must be taken to cook cornstarch well or it will taste.

ADDITIONAL RECIPES.

CUSTARDS, CREAMS, ETC.

BOILED CUSTARD.

One quart milk, four eggs, four tablespoonfuls sugar, one saltspoonful salt, one teaspoonful cornstarch, one teaspoonful vanilla. Dissolve the cornstarch in a little of the cold milk, add to the remainder of the quart boiling hot and cook ten minutes. Beat the eggs and sugar together, pour the boiling milk over them and return to the fire to cook until thick enough to mask the spoon, take at once from the fire, set into cold water and stir often until almost cold. Then add the flavoring and strain into the dish from which it is to be served.

For Cocoanut Custard.—Add one cup grated cocoanut after straining.

For Chocolate Custard.—Melt one ounce of chocolate over hot water, rub well with a little of the hot custard and add before straining.

TIPSY PUDDING.

Half fill a deep dish with any light dry cake, mix one-half cup wine and one-half cup boiling water and pour over it. Just before serving cover with ice cold boiled custard, and garnish with candied cherries or any bright colored jelly.

BAKED CUSTARD.

Make the raw custard as above, using six eggs instead of four and omitting the corn starch. Strain into a mold or cups, set into a deep pan and fill two-thirds of the way to the top of the mold with boiling water. Bake in a very moderate oven. Test often with a knife and take out the instant the knife blade comes out smooth and clean. These two receipts are the foundation for numberless varieties of desserts, according to the fancy of the cook.

SPANISH CREAM.

One quart milk, one-half package gelatine, one cup sugar, one-half teaspoonful salt, four egg yolks, one teaspoonful vanilla. Soak gelatine until very soft in one cup cold water, then drain off all the water that has not been absorbed, boil the milk and add other ingredients, cooking the eggs only two minutes; pour boiling hot onto the gelatine and strain into mold to cool. It should stand at least six hours on ice; whip whites of eggs to a stiff froth, add two tablespoonfuls sugar and flavor to taste. Use to garnish the cream. Rs. Campbell.

BAVARIAN CREAM.

Whip one pint cream to a stiff froth; it ought to make two quarts; if too rich to whip add a little milk. With one scant cup sugar add one-half box gelatine softened in cold water, the yolks of four eggs and one teaspoonful vanilla. Cook one minute and strain into a broad pan set in ice water. Watch it carefully and as soon as it begins to thicken add the whipped cream, folding it in as for an omelet. Put into molds and set on ice to harden. This, too, is the foundation for a large variety of creams.

Coffee Bavarian Cream.—Use one cup clear strong coffee and one cup milk to make the custard.

Chocolate.—Add one ounce chocolate, melted, to the hot custard before straining.

Peach.—Take one pint sifted pulp instead of one pint milk and omit the eggs.

Strawberry, or any Other Small Fruit.—Three pints berries mashed fine, strain the juice, add one cup sugar, gelatine soaked as above and dissolved in one cup boiling water. Add whipped cream and mold as before.

MACAROON CREAM.

Line a deep glass dish with macaroons, putting a bit of raspberry or other jam on each. Make one pint boiled custard (p. 65), strain hot over the macaroons and set away to cool. Just before serving add one pint cream whipped light, stirring a part into the custard and piling the rest on top.

PINEAPPLE SPONGE.

One box gelatine, three pints cold water, one pound white sugar, juice of three lemons, one can grated pineapple, soak gelatine in part of the water till very soft, add remainder of water boiling hot, sugar and lemon juice, let come to the boil, strain and add the pineapple. *Stir well when just beginning to stiffen*, and pour into molds to set. Served with whipped cream.

Mrs. LEDYARD SMITH.

SWEET PUREE OF CHESTNUTS.

Thirty large French chestnuts, one-half cup of sugar, three pints whipped and drained cream, one gill (one-half cup) water, one tablespoonful wine, two tablespoonfuls powdered sugar, shell the chestnuts, boil rapidly for ten minutes in water to cover well, then remove the thin brown skins and return to the fire with water enough to barely cover and boil till so tender that they will crush between the thumb and finger. Drain, pound and sift them, boil the one-half cup sugar in one-half cup water till it will spin, add sifted chestnut and cook about ten minutes until the puree is firm, press through a potato-ricer in a circle on a flat glass dish, being careful not to press it down. Set away to cool till serving time, heap the whipped and flavored cream in the center and serve with wafers. Baked sweet potatoes may be substituted for the chestnuts if very dry and mealy but they will usually need a little more sugar.

MISS PARLOA.

ADDITIONAL RECIPES.

Ice Creams, Sherbets, Etc.

(Directions for Freezing.)

A freezer holding four quarts is the most satisfactory size for family use, and it is well worth while to invest in a crown ice chip at the same time. The hole for draining away water should be about three-quarter of the distance from bottom to top and should never be plugged lest the water rise high enough to enter the can. About ten quarts of fine ice and three pints coarse salt will be needed for a gallon freezer. Diamond C rock salt is the best grade to use, and if drained from the water and dried can be made to serve for several successive freezings. After adjusting the can in the freezer pack fine ice about five inches deep at the bottom. Sprinkle this with one cup of salt and add another layer of ice, alternate salt and ice till even with top of can, packing it down solid with a stick every time salt is added. Pour on one quart cold water and begin turning the handle, slowly at first but after five minutes as fast as convenient, in order to insure a fine smooth cream. More salt will freeze it quicker, but the cream will be coarse grained or even lumpy. Remove the beater as soon as the cream is frozen and work the frozen mass together with a spoon. Cover closely, corking the hole in the cover and if it is to stand very long, repack with fresh ice and salt. Cover the whole freezer with a blanket or piece of carpet and set in a cool place, tipping it slightly to let the extra water run from the drainage hole.

At serving time, lift out the can, hold for two or three minutes under the cold water faucet, wipe dry and turn quickly on to a napkin folded on an ice cold platter.

To keep over night or for several hours, cut a strip of cloth an inch wide, spread it with soft butter and wrap around the joints where the cover fits the mold, drawing as tight as possible and lapping the ends well. This will keep out salt water.

ICE CREAM.

Whip and drain one pint cream, to the thin part that drains from the whip, add one scant cup sugar, one cup cream, one cup milk, and scald thoroughly. Cool and add one tablespoonful vanilla or any flavoring preferred, freeze till like soft mush, then put in the whip and turn the freezer as fast as possible for five minutes; pack and let stand thirty minutes before serving.

This is the best and simplest way to make it, if you can get cream.

COFFEE ICE CREAM.

One quart of cream, three-quarter pound of sugar, one-half pint of strong coffee, mix thoroughly and freeze.

ICE CREAM, NO. 2.

One pint milk, two eggs, one cup sugar, one pint cream (or less), one level tablespoonful flour, one-half cup sugar, one saltspoonful salt, one tablespoonful flavoring. Boil the milk, mix the sugar, flour and salt and stir into it. Cook twenty minutes, stirring constantly; pour boiling hot onto two well-beaten eggs, beating well. Strain, add cream, sugar and flavoring and freeze as usual.

GELATINE ICE CREAM.

One quart cream, one pint milk, one tablespoonful vanilla, one cup sugar, one-eighth package Andrew's gelatine soaked till perfectly soft and then drained; one-half saucespoonful salt. Scald the milk and sugar, pour boiling-hot water over the gelatine, add salt, strain and cool. Whip the cream, add it to the milk and freeze as usual. This has the merit of packing easily into fancy forms and holding its shape in a warm room better than pure cream.

FRUIT CREAMS are made by using one pint of any kind of fruit juice and pulp in place of the milk, changing the proportion of sugar as the fruit is more or less acid. Add from one cup to one pint of cream when partly frozen. Peach cream is improved by adding a few drops of bitter almond.

STRAWBERRY MOUSSE.—Put one pint strawberries through a potato-ricer, add one cup sugar and let them stand for two hours (less will do). Soak one-eighth of a box of Andrew's gelatine in one-quarter cup cold water, whip and drain cream enough to make three pints after draining. Pack a two-quart mold in a freezing mixture, using twice as much salt as usual. Strain the crushed strawberries, add enough boiling water to the gelatine to dissolve it, strain it into the fruit juice and set in ice water till it begins to thicken, then add the whipped cream stirring gently until smooth and evenly mixed. Turn it into the mold, lay over it a sheet of soft white paper, press the cover down close and seal with a buttered strip of cloth or paper. Add salt and ice to cover the mold and let stand for at least four hours. At serving time wipe the mold with a hot cloth to remove any bits of butter and serve on a flat dish. It should cut in smooth slices and show a mossy texture. All fruit mousses are made in the same way. Coffee and caramel mousses are better if the yolk of an egg be well beaten and added to the hot coffee or hot caramel syrup before adding the gelatine; allow one egg for each quart of cream.

BISCUIT ICE CREAM.

One quart whipped and drained cream, two eggs, one-half cup sugar, one-half cup boiling water, one teaspoonful vanilla extract. Boil sugar and water together till it will spin, then pour slowly over beaten whites of eggs, whisking rapidly all the time. Add the beaten yolks and cook over hot water for ten minutes, beating steadily all the time. Set away to cool, add the whipped cream when cold and vanilla, pack and freeze like mousse, allowing four to six hours to freeze. This is much nicer to be flavored with Maraschins, Chartreuse, Abricotine, or some other cordial, and it looks handsomer to have the mold lined with a sherbet of contrasting color.

The addition of dried and powdered macaroons, chopped almonds and French fruit makes what is called Biscuit Tortoni.

SHERBETS are made of fruit juice, sugar and water. The proportions are usually one pint of sugar to one quart water, boiled twenty minutes, then add one pint of any kind of fruit juice and freeze. The addition of one tablespoonful of gelatine soaked till soft and dissolved in the boiling syrup, gives a light, creamy sherbet that seems much richer than the plain. Almost all fruit juice needs the addition of lemon juice to give life to the sherbet.

LEMON SHERBET.

One cup lemon juice, two lumps sugar rubbed on lemon rind, one scant pint sugar, one quart water.

ROMAN PUNCH.

Make lemon sherbet as above, add the juice of one large orange, one tablespoonful gelatine, and when frozen beat in four tablespoonfuls sherry, one gill champagne, one tablespoonful rum and freeze for one-half hour before serving. This is much harder to freeze than a sherbet or cream.

ROMAN PUNCH, NO. 2.

One quart water, one pint sugar, juice of six lemons and one orange, one-quarter cup green tea, two tablespoonfuls rum.

SORBET.—Make any kind of sherbet, and half freeze it. Serve in glasses before or after the roast for a simple sorbet.

A much finer one is made by mixing several kinds of fruit, as one pint chopped pineapple, one-half cup lemon juice, one cup orange juice; or one-half cup shaddock and one cup currant juice.

GRANITES are a kind of rough sorbet and should be frozen without much beating or stirring, as the design is to have a rough icy mixture. They are served either plain or with some kind of cordial beaten in and may come before or after the roast.

FROZEN FRUITS are not to be frozen hard, they should never be kept in the freezer over two hours and a much less time is usually sufficient. They may take the place of a punch or sorbet in the middle of a dinner or at the beginning of a fashionable lunch or breakfast.

FRESH FRUITS.

Strawberries are so often gritty that it seems almost necessary to wash them; to do this with the least possible damage to the berry, put them into a large wire basket, shake it gently in deep cold water, then hang the basket to drain the berries.

Do not hull until needed for the table. Large fine berries are often served with the stem on, when of course a small bowl of sugar must also be served to each person. Each berry is dipped in the sugar and bitten from the stem.

Grapes, currants and cherries are good arranged on a dish of broken ice.

Nuts when to go with raisins are served in the shells, cracked. Salt should always be on the table with nuts of any kind.

Almonds are salted, or fried in sugar, or roasted, glazed, or caramelized and may be served alone with coffee and crackers, with sweet wafers or with raisins or figs according to the whim of the hostess.

Preserved Ginger, chestnut paste or conserve of rose leaves are especially nice to serve with black coffee, wafers and cheese.

ADDITIONAL RECIPES.

SOUP.

The two great divisions of soup made with meat, and soup made without, or purées of vegetables, are really all that there is to learn about soup-making, as if one can make a strong, clear, well-flavored stock and a smooth, creamy, well-seasoned foundation for a purée, all other varieties of soup are only different combinations of the same ingredients, with a different flavor to suit the demand for something new. A number of proved receipts are given for the benefit of those who have had little or no practice.

PLAIN BROWN SOUP STOCK.

Six pounds shin of beef in the proportion of four pounds lean meat to two pounds bone, gristle, etc., six quarts cold water, one-half a chili (red pepper), two whole cloves, one tablespoonful mixed herbs, six peppercorns, one large onion, one tablespoonful salt, two stalks parsley, one carrot, two stalks celery, one turnip. Wipe the meat with a wet cloth, cut it from the bone and into thin slices across the grain. Reserve several of the largest slices with all the marrow, put remainder of meat and bones into six quarts of cold water with the spices and herbs. Set one side of the fire, where it will be at least an hour in coming to the boil. If convenient broil the reserved slices till very brown before adding; if not, fry them in the marrow, being very careful not to let the fat scorch. Brown the chopped vegetables in the same fat before adding them to the soup. Simmer eight to ten hours and strain. The next day remove the fat and use the stock plain for a beef broth or with macaroni or vermicelli, rice, vegetables, etc., according to taste.

CLEAR SOUP STOCK OF CONSOMMÉ.

Add four pounds knuckle of veal or a small fowl to the above rule, with two ounces lean ham or a bone of bacon. Brown only the vegetables, in order to have the soup light colored. After removing the fat add the beaten white and shell of one egg to each quart of jelly, with one saltspoonful celery seed, a few bits of lemon rind, one teaspoonful lemon juice. Mix well together, bring to a boil as quickly as possible, stirring very often. Simmer ten minutes more, strain through a thick napkin and heat to the boiling point before serving. It should be sparkling clear and of a light brown or straw color.

SUMMER JULIENNE.

One quart consommé, one-half cup cooked onion cut in rings, one-half cup of cooked peas, one-half cup asparagus tips, one-half cup cooked string beans, salt and pepper if needed. Heat the vegetables and put them into the tureen; pour boiling soup over them.

WINTER JULIENNE.

One quart of brown stock, one-half teaspoonful salt, one pint mixed vegetables, one-half saltspoonful pepper. Cut the celery and turnip into dice, carrot into match-shaped pieces. Use only the very smallest onions, which should be cut in halves, so that the layers will separate in cups. Cabbage should be coarsely chopped. Cook the vegetables in boiling salted water till tender, but not broken. Drain them and add to the soup a few minutes before serving. Macaroni, vermicelli, rice, tapioca, sago and barley should all be cooked till tender in boiling salted water before adding to the soup, and then allowed to simmer a few minutes to season through.

OXTAIL SOUP.

Wash and cut up two oxtails, separating them at the joints. Select about half of the largest and nicest joints to brown in hot fat before cooking. Simmer in enough water to cover well until perfectly tender. Take out the browned joints and boil the rest to rags; strain, cool and remove fat. Reheat this stock, adding one quart strong brown stock, more salt and pepper if needed, and the reserved joints. It should be served boiling hot.

LEFT OVER SOUP.

Bones and trimmings from a roast of beef, beefsteak bones and trimmings, mutton chop bones, any cold vegetables except squash, cold cooked eggs in any shape, crusts of bread. There should be about six pounds of meat altogether; add whatever gravy was left over and four quarts cold water; add one-half teaspoonful celery seed, one tablespoonful salt, one clove, four peppercorns, and simmer eight or ten hours till the meat is in rags and the water reduced one-half. Strain and set away for stock.

Glaze is simply clear stock boiled down to one-eighth its original amount. It should be almost like glue in consistency and will keep two months if closely covered in a cool place. Put it away in small jelly pots or tumblers, so as to open only a part at a time. It is invaluable for strengthening weak soups, making gravies and browning boiled or steamed meats to look and taste like roasts.

CALF'S HEAD OR MOCK TURTLE.

One calf's head cleaned with the skin on, cut in halves, and well washed in salt and water. Remove the brains and tie them in coarse muslin to be cooked separately; boil in four quarts of water till the meat is tender and ready to slip from the bones. Lay the meat flat on a platter, return bones to the pot and boil till the water is reduced to two quarts, then strain and cool. Remove fat and return to the fire with two quarts rich brown stock, two whole cloves, a blade of mace, six allspice berries, one chili, more salt if needed. While this is simmering cut the meat and tongue into dice; there should be a generous pint; chop the trimmings to a paste; cook the brains twenty minutes and pound with the chopped meat; season with salt, pepper and thyme; add a little beaten egg to bind it well together and shape in balls size of a large hickory nut and fry them brown in a little butter. Brown four tablespoonfuls flour in two tablespoonfuls butter or bacon fat and add hot soup to it slowly, stirring well till smooth; add it to the stock. Put meat balls and diced meat into a hot tureen and strain the boiling stock over them. As one head is enough for a gallon of soup it will pay to put a part of it into glass jars exactly as you would fruit. This is usually served with a glass of sherry wine in the soup, but it is equally good with thin slices of lemon and a tablespoonful of mushroom catsup, if you only think so.

SOUPS WITHOUT STOCK.

(Foundation for soups made with milk.)

One quart milk, one tablespoonful butter, one teaspoonful chopped onion, one-half tablespoonful flour, one stalk celery, one teaspoonful salt, one-half saltspoonful white pepper, speck of cayenne, one-half teaspoonful celery salt. Cook milk, onion and celery twenty minutes in double boiler; cook the flour and butter together five minutes, being careful not to brown it, then pour it into the soup; add the seasoning and it is ready to finish in any way.

POTATO SOUP.—Add three boiled potatoes, mashed very fine, to the foundation; rub through a sieve into hot tureen.

CELERY SOUP.—Add one pint stewed and sifted celery to the foundation and strain over one egg beaten to a cream, stirring well.

MOCK BISQUE.

Simmer one-half quart can of tomatoes till very soft, strain it and pour into the foundation after the latter has been strained into the tureen. Most palates prefer the addition of one-half teaspoonful sugar to the tomatoes.

OYSTER SOUP.

Prepare foundation, omitting onion and celery, and using two tablespoonfuls flour. Put one quart oysters in a large bowl and pour over them one cup water; take out each oyster with the fingers to make sure no shell adheres to it and drain in the colander. Strain the oyster liquor through the finest strainer, put it on to boil and skim well; add the oysters and simmer till they grow plump and begin to curl on the edges. Add oysters to foundation with as much of the broth as will make it of the right consistency. Add more salt and pepper if needed and all the butter it will bear without floating on the top. Crackers browned in the oven are good with this soup.

ADDITIONAL RECIPES.

ADDITIONAL RECIPES.

FISH.

Fish with dark meat are generally richer and of higher flavor than those with white meat, and on that account should be chosen for boiling and steaming, never for frying, though they are good when panned and baked.

TO BOIL A 4-LB. FISH.

Put into your fish-kettle one level tablespoonful salt, six peppercorns, two stems parsley, one carrot and one onion each cut fine, one cup sour white wine, one pint water. Lay fish on the drainer, cover with a buttered paper, set to boil and simmer forty minutes, or more if the flesh does not part easily from the bones at the end of that time. Strain the water in which it was cooked and use with four tablespoonfuls butter and one tablespoonful flour to make a white sauce, thicken with one well-beaten egg and add one tablespoonful of Soyer's or any other tablesauce, one tablespoonful lemon juice and more pepper and salt if needed. The wine can be replaced by a little weak vinegar or lemon juice.

DARNE OF SALMON

Is the middle cut; there are but two, or sometimes three from a large fish. Lay in a stew pan on a bed of sliced carrots and onions, parsley and peppercorns; dredge lightly with salt and pour over one pint claret, one pint thin broth, dot with three tablespoonfuls butter and cover with a buttered paper. Bring quickly to a boil and simmer very gently one hour. Drain and remove the skin, mask with a remoulade sauce made by rubbing well together the yolks of two hard-boiled eggs with one raw, one teaspoonful mustard, one-half teaspoonful salt, one-half saltspoonful white pepper, one teaspoonful chopped parsley. Add two tablespoonfuls vinegar and beat in by degrees one-half pint oil alternating with more vinegar until three tablespoonfuls of tarragon vinegar have been used, beat with Dover beater till very light and thick. The liquor in which the fish is cooked can be strained and used several times.

BROILED FISH.

Large broiled fish should be split through the back, and for most stoves the head and tail must be removed. Use a double wire broiler and grease it well before laying in the fish. Dust the fish with salt and pepper and broil the flesh side first till almost done, then cook on the skin side just long enough to brown it well. Small fish require from five to ten minutes. Thick ones from fifteen to twenty minutes. Turn an old dripping-pan over the broiler and it will cook more evenly. There is no excuse for scorching the fish, as one can always scatter a few ashes over a hot fire. Spread generously with butter and set in the warming-oven a minute to let it penetrate the fish. Garnish with parsley or water-cress after taking from the oven.

BAKED WHITE FISH OR TROUT.

Choose a fish weighing about six pounds and have the head left on. Clean carefully, letting boiling water run through the mouth and eye sockets. Gash the skin at intervals of two inches and lay in narrow slips of salt pork. Rub the fish with salt, pepper, soft butter and dredge lightly with flour. Skewer it in O or S shape and lay on bed of pork chips on a fish sheet. Put into a hot oven without water in the dripping-pan. Baste often with the fat from the pork or a little melted butter. Serve on a folded napkin, garnishing with parsley and Saratoga chips piled about the fish.

STUFFING.—One cup of coarse cracker crumbs, one saltspoonful salt, one saltspoonful pepper, one-half teaspoonful chopped onion, one teaspoonful chopped parsley, one teaspoonful capers, one teaspoonful chopped pickle, melted butter enough to moisten.

SMALL FISH BAKED.

Lay in a baking dish with chopped onion, mushrooms and parsley, rub the fish with salt, pepper, a bit of nutmeg and dot with butter. Pour in enough thin broth to cover bottom of dish, add a glass of sour wine and bake till the flesh parts easily from the bone.

PANNED FISH.

This is suitable for very small fish or such as can be cut in slices. Have the fish well cleaned, seasoned with pepper and salt and dried with a little flour, or better still, very fine bread crumbs. Have a large frying pan smoking hot with as little grease in it as will keep the fish from sticking. Dripping from good, sweet salt pork is the best, but any sweet dripping will do. When the fat begins to smoke blue, lay in the fish and brown quick on both sides, then cover closely and set back to cook more slowly, from ten to twenty minutes, according to the size of the fish.

FRIED FISH.

Fish for frying should be thoroughly dried after cleaning, seasoned with salt and pepper, rolled in fine bread crumbs, then dipped in beaten egg, then rolled in crumbs again, fry in deep fat like doughnuts; put in only a few pieces at a time to avoid chilling the fat and let it reheat before frying any more. The temperature should not fall below 375 deg. From two to five minutes is sufficient for any but extra large pieces. The fish is done when it rises to the top of the fat. Drain perfectly dry on paper and arrange on a folded napkin. Fry the parsley that is to garnish the dish, taking care to have it crisp, without changing its color.

FISH AU GRATIN.

Six pounds of any fish with white meat, steamed, freed from skin and bone and broken into flakes. One pint of cream sauce No. 1, and one cup cracker crumbs moistened with melted butter; put a layer of fish in a gratin dish, season well with salt, pepper, cayenne and celery salt, and sprinkle with chopped parsley, pour over a part of the cream sauce, repeat till the fish is all used, reserving most of the sauce to pour over the top; sprinkle buttered crumbs over the top and bake in a rather quick oven until it boils up in the middle and the crumbs are brown.

FISH SALAD.

Break cold cooked halibut into convenient pieces, removing all skin, bones and fat, marinate with tarragon or spiced vinegar and set one side for an hour; arrange on leaves of lettuce and serve with Mayonnaise or sauce tartare.

CREAMED SALT FISH.

Serve one cup shredded salt fish in cream sauce No. 2, page 109, in a potato border.

SANTÉED OYSTERS.

Wash and pick over one pint oysters, add one pint stale bread crumbs, salt and pepper to taste, add one egg beaten lightly; let them stand fifteen minutes, then lay by tablespoonfuls into a frying pan with a little hot butter; brown well on both sides and serve as soon as possible.

PANNED OYSTERS.

Put one tablespoonful butter in a covered saucepan with one-half saltspoonful of white pepper, one teaspoonful salt, and a few grains of cayenne, when hot add one pint of washed and drained oysters, cover closely and shake the pan to keep them from sticking; cook about three minutes or until plump. Serve on toasted bread or crackers.

SCALLOPED OYSTERS.

Wash oysters in their own liquor, then put a layer of them in a deep dish, strew over them a thick layer of cracker dust, a little butter, season as you prefer, and spread butter over, then another layer of oysters and so on until the dish is full. Set them in the oven and bake to a light brown.   S.

CLAM BROTH.

Twenty-five clams washed and drained, steam till the shells open easily; save every drop of juice that comes with opening and add enough water to make one quart. With a pair of scissors trim off the soft part of the clam and reserve to serve with the broth. Chop the tough portion a little and simmer fifteen minutes in the broth. Strain and add pepper and salt if needed, and serve in very small bouillon cups. Send the reserved portion to the table with melted butter and lemon juice poured over them.

LOBSTERS.

Choose one that feels heavy in proportion to its size; the claws should be darker than the body, if they are spotted with black some judges think it shows a richer flavor, especially see that the tail is stiff and elastic so that when bent out it springs back at once; otherwise they were dead before boiling. Lobsters boiled when dead are watery and soft, and are so unwholesome that it is dangerous to eat them. Separate the tail from the body and twist off all the claws; shake out carefully the tom-ally (this is the liver of the lobster and is of a greenish color) also the coral if there is any. Draw the body from the shell, remove the stomach and throw it away with the head. Split the body and pick every scrap of meat from between the fine bones, cut the under side of the tail-shell, loosen the meat and take it out in one piece. Split the meat open to remove a little vein running its entire length. This is sometimes white, sometimes red or black, but must always be carefully taken out and thrown away. Shave off the outer edge of the claws, and then it is easy to remove the meat without tearing it. To serve plain boiled lobster, arrange the meat in the center of a cold platter. Garnish the edges with heart leaves of lettuce, and the claws; send to the table with a cut lemon, and let each one season for himself with salt, pepper, mustard, vinegar and oil.

DEVILED LOBSTER.

Two cups finely diced lobster meat, salt and cayenne to taste, yolks of four hard-boiled eggs, one tablespoonful chopped parsley, a speck of nutmeg, one cup of thick cream sauce. Add lobster, eggs mashed fine, parsley and seasoning to the sauce while it is hot. Fill the sections of lobster shell and dust with buttered cracker crumbs. Brown in the hottest kind of an oven and serve very hot. A tablespoonful of Worcestershire or Mushroom catsup is an improvement for those who like it very highly seasoned.

LOBSTER WITH CECIL SAUCE.

Cut the meat of a three-pound lobster into inch bits. Put one tablespoonful butter into a frying pan and mix with it one tablespoonful flour; add slowly one-half cup cream, one-half cup stock, the lobster with salt and pepper to taste. Let boil up thoroughly then take from the fire and stir in the beaten yolk of one egg and one tablespoonful of chopped parsley. This may be served in paper cases or individual dishes.

LOBSTER NEWBURG.

Cut the meat of two small lobsters into small thin slices and cook them slowly in four tablespoonfuls of butter for five minutes. Then add one teaspoonful of salt, one saltspoonful pepper, a speck of cayenne, two tablespoonfuls each of brandy and sherry, a dash of mace and simmer five minutes longer. Beat well the yolks of four eggs, mix with them one cup cream and pour it over the cooking mixture. Stir constantly for one and one-half minutes, then serve quickly in a warm dish. Garnish with triangles of puff-paste.

PETITES SAUFFLÉES D'HOMARD.

Dice a two-pound lobster, showing the red side as much as possible. Put bands of writing paper, about two inches high, around as many individual ramequin cases as you wish to serve. Beat three tablespoonfuls of stiff Mayonnaise, one cup Aspic jelly, one-half cup tomato sauce together until they begin to look white, then stir in the pieces of lobster adding a very little tarragon vinegar or better still one teaspoonful chopped tarragon and put away to stiffen in a very cold place. When set take off the papers carefully, garnish with pounded coral or browned crumbs.

SOFT SHELL CRABS.

Lift each point of the back shell, and remove the spongy substance found beneath it, taking care to scrape and cut away every bit. Turn the crab on its back, and remove the semi-circular piece of dark, soft shell called the "apron" or "flap" and more of the same spongy substance lying under it. Wash in cold water and dry carefully on a towel. Season with salt and pepper, dip in egg and roll in crumbs. Fry about three minutes in very hot fat, putting in only two at a time, as they should be ice-cold when prepared. Serve with Tartar sauce.

BAKED CRABS.

After cleaning and seasoning, dip them into melted butter and sprinkle thickly with grated bread crumbs. Range on a dripping-pan and set into an intensely hot oven for about five minutes. Serve with horseradish cream sauce.

BROILED CRABS.

Prepare as above, but cook in a double broiler over clear hot coals for eight to ten minutes. Serve with melted butter and lemon juice poured over.

ADDITIONAL RECIPES.

Roasting and Braising.

For all roasting and braising the heat should be greatest at first, to harden the surface of the meat and retain its juice. Baste well with its own fat before adding any water. The meat should be raised at least an inch and a half from the bottom of the baking pan. There are racks made expressly for the purpose. Reduce the heat after the first twenty or thirty minutes and allow twelve minutes to the pound for beef and mutton, fifteen minutes for lamb and veal, thirty minutes for pork.

ROAST BEEF.

One of the best pieces for roasting is the tip of the sirloin. Have the backbone trimmed very close; cut the ribs close to the solid part of the meat and remove them from the flank part. Roll the flank end toward the backbone and with a large needle and twine secure it by two or three stitches through the tough skin. Do not wash, but sponge with a wet cloth; rub lightly with pepper and salt and dredge on flour enough to dry the surface. Put plenty in the bottom of the pan if a brown gravy is wished. Lay on the rack with the serving-side down at first. If the oven is hot enough it will need to be turned in about an hour. Watch carefully, basting every fifteen minutes, and as soon as well browned on all sides pour in enough water to cover the bottom of the pan. Let the water cook away toward the last, so that the fat can be poured away. After the meat is done set it into a hot closet, but do not cover while making gravy. Add one pint hot water to the sediment left in pan after the fat has been poured off. Place on the stove and scrape all the glaze from bottom and side of the pan. When it boils add a thickening made of two teaspoonfuls of flour, rubbed smooth with four tablespoonfuls of cold water, pouring it in slowly, as it is not possible to know just how much the browned flour already in the pan will help to thicken it. Boil well, add salt and pepper to taste, and strain into a hot dish.

ROAST MUTTON.

Roast mutton is cooked in the same way, but the piece chosen is usually the leg or loin. The leg is greatly improved by having the bone removed and filling its place with a stuffing made of one coffee cup coarse cracker crumbs, one teaspoonful salt, one saltspoonful pepper, one teaspoonful mint, dried and powdered; moisten with melted butter.

ROAST VEAL.

Roast veal should have a stuffing made of stale bread, grated. Season highly, allowing one teaspoonful salt, one saltspoonful pepper, one-half teaspoonful thyme, a few drops onion juice, one teaspoonful lemon juice, and the yolk of one raw egg to each scant pint of crumbs. Moisten with melted butter. The gravy of veal is improved by adding to it one tablespoonful of grated horse-radish.

ROAST PORK.

Many persons like a flavor of sage; in that case sift a teaspoonful of it, finely powdered, over the meat when it is ready for the oven.

ROAST VENISON.

Unless very young and tender, venison is apt to be hard and dry unless larded or protected by a thick covering of flour paste. This is as satisfactory a method as any. Wipe the meat carefully and draw off the dry skin; lard the lean sides, using about one-half pound of clear fat salt pork; rub all over with soft butter, then dredge with salt, pepper and flour, being generous with the flour. Lay the meat on the rack in the dripping pan and sprinkle flour in the pan with two tablespoonfuls of diced pork. Watch carefully till the flour in the pan is brown, which should be in five minutes. Now add boiling water enough to cover the bottom of the pan and close the oven door. In fifteen minutes begin to baste with the gravy from the pan and baste every ten minutes, renewing the water often, as it boils away. At the end of an hour add one-half pint claret to the gravy and let the last basting be with soft butter and flour. Drain off all the fat from the gravy and add one-half tumbler of currant jelly, melted, but do not thicken the gravy for game. One and one-half hours is enough for a leg weighing ten pounds.

ROAST HAM.

Wash and scrape carefully and soak in cold water twenty-four hours. Scrape again and dry thoroughly. Make a dough with two quarts of flour and water enough for a stiff paste. Roll this into a sheet large enough to wrap the ham; fold the ham in it and place on a meat rack in the dripping pan. Bake in a moderate oven six hours. On taking from the oven remove the paste and skin, sprinkle with fine crumbs and return to the oven for half an hour. Dust very carefully with cayenne and baste every five minutes with wine, using one cup claret and two tablespoonfuls sherry. It will be delicious either hot or cold, and is especially nice if served hot with champagne sauce.

BRAISING.

Braising is particularly adapted for meats that are lacking in flavor or are tough. A deep pan with a close fitting cover are necessary; granite ware is the most satisfactory for small ones, while larger ones should be made of Russia iron with folded seams, as both pan and cover must be without solder.

BRAISED BEEF.

Trim a piece weighing about four pounds into a smooth shape; lard it on each side with three or four pieces of salt pork; let it marinate for twelve hours in the juice of one lemon, one tablespoonful salad oil, one tablespoonful salt, one tablespoonful peppercorn, a sprig each of thyme and parsley. Brown the meat well on all sides in a frying-pan, then lay it in the braising pan on a bed of chopped onion, carrot and parsley; pour in boiling water to half cover and cook in a moderate oven two hours or more until very tender; turn once in the time; lift the meat onto a hot platter; skim the fat from the gravy and skim out the vegetables to serve with the meat if liked. Thicken the gravy with one heaping tablespoonful of flour and strain it over the meat. This dish is often served with a garnishing of several different kinds of vegetables cooked separately in clear water and arranged around it.

FRICAUDEAU OF VEAL.

Cut a block weighing about three pounds from the leg; remove the sinews and lard the top with rather small strips of salt pork. Brown it lightly in a frying pan and lay on a bed of one sliced carrot, one sliced onion and a bouquet. Season with one scant tablespoonful salt, a dust of pepper; cover the bottom of the pan with white broth and cook in a braising pan for one and one-half hours, basting occasionally. Serve with one-half pint pureé of spinach on the dish, placing the veal on top.

CALF'S LIVER.

Calf's liver is braised in the same way, except that sweet herbs are added to the broth, and just before serving one-half pint of Spanish sauce is poured over it. It will cook in forty-five minutes. Strain the thickened gravy over and garnish with small boiled onions.

SWEETBREADS BRAISED.

Take six blanched sweetbreads, lard the upper side slightly and sauté them with some bits of fat pork; add one-half cupful each of sliced onion and carrot and a bouquet; dredge with salt and flour and shake until a golden brown, then moisten with one pint strong white stock. Cover with a buttered paper and cook in a hot oven forty minutes, lifting the paper often to baste them. They will then be ready to serve with any desired sauce.

ADDITIONAL RECIPES.

ADDITIONAL RECIPES.

ENTRÉES.

BEEF-STEAK PIE.

Cut two and one-half pounds steak into small pieces with a very little fat, dip each piece into flour, place them in a pie dish, season each layer with pepper, salt and a very little cayenne pepper, fill the dish sufficiently with slices of steak to raise the crust in the middle, half fill the dish with water or any gravy left from roast beef, and one tablespoonful of Worcestershire sauce, put a border of paste around the wet edge of the pie dish, moisten it and lay the crust over it, cut the paste even with the dish, butter top and bake.

One cup tomatoes makes a very nice addition if there be not sufficient gravy or stock.　　　　　　　　　　　　　　　S.

CHICKEN POT PIE.

Divide the chicken into pieces at the joints, boil until part done, or about twenty minutes, then take it out, fry two or three slices of fat salt pork and put in the bottom, then place the chicken on with one cup of water, two ounces of butter, one teaspoonful of salt, pepper to taste and cover the top with a light crust, the same as for biscuit. Bake in an oven that is hotter at the top than at the bottom, and when well risen and brown cover with a paper or the crust will burn before the pie is baked through. Remove fat from the water in which the chicken was boiled, thicken with a little flour, season to taste, add one cup good cream and when the pie is done pour this gravy through the holes of the crust.　　　　　　　　　　　　　　　　S.

HOW TO BROIL A STEAK.

A steak should be evenly cut about three-quarters of an inch thick, if cut any thicker it is apt to be brown on the outside, while still uncooked inside. Do not wash the steak, take a wet cloth and wipe or rather mop it, but do not pour water on it. Whatever cooks may urge in favor of pounding a steak, it is not good; it breaks the cells of the meat in which the gravy is contained; if there is a tough piece on the steak it may be hacked a little with the back of a knife. Heat the broiler, wipe with a clean cloth, just before using, rub the bars with suet to prevent from marking the meat and watch constantly to keep from burning, smoking or catching fire, lifting it up when necessary, but do no turning until the one side is nicely browned; then turn to the other side, then turn once more, that is, twice for each side, season with pepper and salt and pour a little melted butter on top. S.

ROAST GOOSE.

Geese and ducks, if old, are better if parboiled before they are roasted. Put them on in sufficient water to cover them and simmer about two hours. Make a stuffing with four onions, one ounce green sage chopped fine, a large cupful of stale bread crumbs and the same of mashed potatoes, one cup raisins, one cup of fine chopped apples, one teaspoonful of butter, one teaspoonful salt, pepper, two eggs, mix well together and stuff the body of the goose, then place in a good hot oven and bake about one hour and a half, and serve apple sauce with it. S.

STUFFING FOR TURKEY.

Mix thoroughly one quart of stale bread, very finely grated, grate a rind of a lemon, quarter of an ounce of chopped parsley, one onion, a little thyme and season with salt and pepper, then add two eggs, one-half cup of butter, mix all well together and moisten with hot milk. S.

YORKSHIRE PUDDING, HOTEL STYLE.

One quart flour, two heaped teaspoonfuls Star Crystal Baking Powder, one cup butter, one teaspoonful salt, rub butter into the flour, add ice cold water enough to make a short dough, mix light with a spoon, and bake in a hot oven, and serve with roast meats. S.

MINCED BEEF.

Take cold pieces of beef that have been left over, and chop them fine, then add two boiled potatoes, one onion chopped fine, pepper and salt, a little beef broth if handy, put all in a frying pan and cook slowly; a poached egg should be served with it.

MEAT BALLS.

Chop a piece of boiled beef with one onion, season with salt and pepper, add parsley, stale bread crumbs, and flavor with nutmeg; moisten it with an egg, mix well, form into small balls, roll in flour, and fry in hot fat.

JUMBALLAYA.

Wash one pound rice and soak it one hour, cut up a cold roast chicken or remnants of turkey and a slice of ham. Toss it lightly in one heaping tablespoonful of butter till slightly browned. Stir in the rice and add slowly one pint hot water or broth, cover closely and set where it can cook slowly till the rice is tender. It is very nice made with oysters or shrimps.

CALF'S BRAIN BREADED.

Separate the two lobes of the brain with a knife, soak them in cold water with a little salt for one hour; then pour away water and cover with hot water, clean and skin them; then dip in egg and milk, roll in bread crumbs and fry slowly in deep hot fat, serve tomato sauce with it.

WELSH RAREBIT.

Take one-half pound cheese (American cheese preferred), three tablespoonfuls ale, a thin slice of toast, grate the cheese fine, put it to the ale, and work it in a small saucepan over a slow fire till it is melted, spread it on toast and serve hot. (If ale is not at hand, use beer or milk.)

ADDITIONAL RECIPES.

EGGS.

BREAKFAST EGGS.

Should never be boiled. A thin shell of the white is made hard and indigestible, while the bulk of the egg is barely warmed through. The following is a better way. Put six into a vessel that will hold two quarts. Fill with boiling water, cover closely and set on the stove shelf for seven minutes to cook very soft; ten minutes for medium, twelve to fifteen minutes for very firm. Crumple a napkin in a hot dish and serve ranged in its folds.

POACHED EGGS.

For six persons allow six eggs, one tablespoonful milk, one saltspoonful salt, a speck of pepper and one-half teaspoonful of butter to each egg. Break the egg into a bowl, add the seasoning but do not beat. When the milk begins to boil pour in the eggs and seasoning. *Do not stir* but as the egg cooks, scrape gently from bottom of the dish, drawing the cooked mass to one side. Remove from fire before it is quite firm through, turn into a hot dish and serve quickly.

SCRAMBLED EGGS.

Are the same as above, but omit the milk.

DROPPED EGGS.

For this the eggs should be new-laid and cold. Put a quart of water, one teaspoonful salt and one teaspoonful vinegar in a shallow pan, arrange in it as many muffin rings as there are eggs to be cooked, and set the pan where the water will bubble at one side only. Break the eggs one at a time and slide them into the rings. If the water does not cover them, gently pour on a little more boiling water till it does. Cook till the white is set over the yolks; then pour off most of the water; with a cake-turner lift each egg and lay on a slice of buttered toast, removing the ring after it is in place.

GRIDDLED EGGS.

Heat the griddle almost as much as for baking cakes, butter it lightly and range small muffin rings on it. Drop an egg in each and turn as soon as lightly browned. They resemble fried eggs, but are far more delicate.

BAKED EGGS.

Make a thin white sauce with one cup milk, one tablespoonful butter, one teaspoonful flour, one-half teaspoonful salt, one-quarter teaspoonful pepper, one teaspoonful chopped parsley. Pour this sauce into a large ramequin dish or deep pie plate and break into it as many eggs as you wish. Bake in a moderate oven till the white is set, *or*, omit the parsley and sprinkle grated cheese over it before baking.

SPANISH EGGS.

Rub the inside of a frying pan with a freshly cut onion, pare one large tomato and cut into small bits, put into the pan one heaping tablespoonful butter, add tomato as soon as it is melted and cook for five minutes, stirring occasionally. Beat the eggs enough to break the yolks and turn them into the hot tomato with one teaspoonful salt, one-half saltspoonful pepper; stir like poached eggs and serve on buttered toast.

BEAUREGARD EGGS.

Cook four eggs twenty minutes, make a white sauce with one cup milk, one tablespoonful butter, one tablespoonful cornstarch; lay six small squares of buttered toast on a dish, cover it with white sauce, then sprinkle with the whites chopped fine, and the yolks pressed through a ricer.

EN MARINADE.

Six hard-boiled eggs, with four whole cloves stuck in each; rub together one-half teaspoonful salt, one-half teaspoonful pepper, one-half teaspoonful mustard with a little cold vinegar; let one pint vinegar come to the boil, add the spice and cook one minute, pour boiling hot over the eggs, in a glass jar, cover closely. They will be ready to use in about two weeks. A few pieces of boiled beet in the vinegar will turn them a pretty pink. These are nice for picnics and lunches, or to accompany broiled beef steak.

PLAIN OMELET.

Put four eggs into a bowl with half a teaspoonful salt, one scant saucespoonful pepper, give them twelve vigorous beats with a fork and add four tablespoonfuls milk or cream; put one teaspoonful butter in an omelet pan, shake it over the fire till frothy, turn in the eggs and shake over a quick fire until they are set; roll and turn on to a dish. To make Jelly, Parsley, Ham, Cheese or Chicken Omelet spread the seasoning over the egg just before rolling it.

OMELET, NO. 2.

For each egg allow one saltspoonful salt, a dust of pepper, one tablespoonful of liquid (milk, cream, stock, tomato, etc.). Break whites and yolks separately, beating each until very light; add seasoning and fold the yolks into the whites, stirring as little as possible. Have the omelet pan hot, melt in it one teaspoonful of butter and cook over a quick fire until well browned on the bottom, then set into the oven until the top is set. Fold carefully not to break the crust, and turn onto a hot dish. Serve at once. This omelet is delicious made with ham, or green peas, or asparagus tips. The latter should be well cooked, drained, seasoned and spread on just before folding the omelet; the ham may be folded in or mixed through the whole egg. Oysters should be parboiled and drained; the liquor from them may be strained and used instead of milk to give a richer flavor to the omelet.

BAKED OMELET.

For six persons use six eggs, one-half c.pful of milk, one tablespoonful of flour, one teaspoonful Star **Crystal Baking Powder,** one teaspoonful salt, one tablespoonful butter; mix the milk and flour, beat whites of eggs to a stiff froth, add the salt and the yolks of the eggs to them and beat enough to mix well. Put the butter in a hot frying pan, add milk, flour and baking powder to the eggs and stir quickly; turn the mixture into the buttered pan and set in a hot oven about ten minutes, or until well set and brown, fold and turn on a dish as usual.

ADDITIONAL RECIPES.

ADDITIONAL RECIPES.

SALADS.

FRENCH DRESSING.

Three tablespoonfuls oil, one-fourth teaspoonful salt, one tablespoonful vinegar, one-half saltspoonful pepper; beat salt, pepper and oil together with a fork, then add the vinegar slowly, beating well. Use at once, as the jelly soon separates.

MAYONNAISE.

Put into a cold bowl the yolks of three eggs and beat with a Dover beater until very light and thick; add one level teaspoonful mustard, one level teaspoonful salt, one saltspoonful sugar, one-half saltspoonful cayenne, and a few drops of oil. Continue beating until too thick to turn the beater easily. Add lemon juice to thin it, alternately with more oil, until two tablespoonfuls have been used; after that add vinegar to the same amount. It will take about one pint of oil to make this amount stiff enough to hold its shape when dropped from a spoon. At the last whip four tablespoonfuls of cream thick and stiff and beat into the sauce. If the sauce is to be kept any length of time do not add the cream until just before using, or omit cream entirely, using just enough oil to make it of the right consistence.

CREAM SALAD DRESSING.

Rub the yolks of three hard-boiled eggs to a smooth paste; add gradually to them one teaspoonful salt, one-fourth teaspoonful sugar, one-half saltspoonful cayenne, one teaspoonful mustard and two tablespoonfuls vinegar; have one pint cream very cold and whip it till thick and smooth; beat this, a tablespoonful at a time, into the mixture with a whisk.

BOILED DRESSING.

Cook one teaspoonful flour in one tablespoonful butter two minutes, pour into it slowly one-half cup of boiling hot vinegar, beating smooth with a wooden spoon; cook five minutes, then pour into it one egg, beaten smooth; cook one minute and set away to cool; thin with cream when ready to use. This is particularly nice for cold slaw, and should be poured hot over the chopped cabbage.

SWEETBREAD SALAD.

Clean and blanch one pair of large sweetbreads (there should be enough to make a pint when diced); marinate them with one tablespoonful of lemon juice, one teaspoonful oil, pepper and salt to taste, and set them on ice for an hour or more. At serving time add an equal bulk of diced celery, enough mayonnaise to moisten well and arrange it in six portions on a bed of lettuce leaves. Drop a teaspoonful of dressing on top of each and garnish with olives cut in spirals.

OYSTER SALAD.

For a one pound can or a solid pint of oysters use the following dressing: Beat well two eggs, add to them one-fourth cup each of cream and vinegar, one-half teaspoonful each of mustard, celery salt and salt, a dust of cayenne, one tablespoonful butter. Put into double boiler and cook like soft custard. Parboil the oysters, drain them and add the dressing. Set away to cool and at serving time add one pint diced celery.

*VEGETABLE SALADS.

Vegetable salads can be made of any kind of cooked vegetables, but some kinds combine better than others. Peas, string or shell beans, cauliflower, asparagus and young carrots combine well, turnips, carrots, beets, cabbage, spinach, tomatoes, make another combination, but it is generally best to use potatoes for the body of the salad, adding other vegetables to give color and flavor. A large variety is known as "Salade Macédoine," or sometimes Russian salad. Each vegetable should be cooked and cut separately, then mixed lightly in a bowl with French dressing and set on ice to cool before serving. Rub the salad bowls with a cut onion before arranging the salad, and if it is liked very moist and highly seasoned, double the quantity of dressing or send a bowl of mayonnaise to the table with it. Garnish with nasturtium in the season and cut them up with the salad. Sliced gherkins, pickled beets, marinated eggs, Thon Mariné make savory garnishes.

SPINACH SALAD.

Press all the water from boiled spinach and mince it fine; toss it with a French dressing and set away to season for an hour; serve with a cream dressing and garnish with strips of white cut from hard boiled eggs and strips of cucumber cut lengthwise; rub the yolks through a strainer and place it in a mound in the center.

STRAWBERRY SALAD.

Choose the heart leaves of head lettuce, heap a few strawberries in each and dust them lightly with powdered sugar; lay a teaspoonful of mayonnaise on each portion and serve cut lemons with them; delicious for lunch.

ORANGE SALAD.

For six persons pare four rather acid oranges, slice them very thin, cutting down the sides instead of across, and sprinkle sparingly with sugar. Mix one tablespoonful sherry with one of yellow Chartreuse and one of lemon juice and pour it over the fruit. Set on ice an hour before using. Serve before the game course.

ANCHOVY SALAD.

Soak twelve Norwegian anchovies over night, drain them and dry by pressing gently in a cloth; remove bone and skin and roll each half in a fillet; lay these on a bed of shredded lettuce; garnish with sliced cucumbers and cut olives and marinate with a French dressing. Serve with sauce tartare made by adding one teaspoonful each of finely chopped parsley, gherkins and capers to one cup very thick mayonnaise.

ADDITIONAL RECIPES.

Meat and Fish Sauces.

The foundation for almost all our common sauces is what the French call a "roux," made as follows:

Melt one ounce (one rounded tablespoonful) butter in a saucepan and let it boil till it begins to show a pale straw color. Add two tablespoonfuls flour and stir briskly. Add one pint hot milk, or milk and water, or water, pouring slowly and beating hard, add one-half teaspoonful salt, one-half saltspoonful white pepper and a speck of cayenne and you have a plain white sauce or drawn butter to which a good tablespoonful of butter should be added just long enough to melt before going to the table.

When the butter and flour are allowed to become brown it is called a brown roux and is used for soups, stews, gravies, etc.

CREAM SAUCE NO. 1.

One pint cream, one-half teaspoonful salt, one tablespoonful butter, one-half saltspoonful pepper, two tablespoonfuls flour, a speck cayenne. Make as above.

CREAM SAUCE NO. 2.

Make as in No. 1, using only one scant tablespoonful flour and thickening with a liaison of two egg yolks beaten with an equal bulk of cold water, return to the sauce pan until the sauce thickens like soft custard.

CREAM SAUCE NO. 3, FOR CROQUETTES, ETC.

Allow two tablespoonfuls butter and four heaping tablespoonfuls flour to a pint of cream, seasoning as before. This sauce is much improved by using half or more rich chicken stock in place of all cream.

VELVET SAUCE.

Melt one ounce butter, add two tablespoonfuls flour and stir well. Moisten with one quart good veal or chicken stock, add a bouquet, one-half cup of mushroom liquor, six whole peppers, one saltspoonful salt, a suspicion of nutmeg. Boil for twenty minutes stirring continuously, then remove to side of fire, skim well, and simmer very slowly one hour. Strain and add more salt and pepper if needed.

SPANISH SAUCE.

Two carrots, one onion, cut fine and cooked in two ounces bacon or sausage dripping, add one sprig thyme, one bay leaf, six peppers, one clove, two sprigs parsley, four stalks celery (or one-quarter teaspoonful celery seed). Two quarts weak white broth of any kind and simmer gently for one-half hour; then add strong brown stock enough to make four quarts.

Boil slowly three hours, adding any bones of roast veal or ham at hand. Strain and put away for constant use. It will keep a month in cold weather and is the foundation for numberless fancy sauces.

MAYONAISE SAUCE.

Two raw egg yolks in an earthen bowl with one-half teaspoonful dry mustard, one-half teaspoonful salt, one-half saltspoonful cayenne. Beat with a Dover beater till very light, then add drop by drop one pint of salad oil beating constantly. If it thickens too much to stir well, put in lemon juice until two tablespoonfuls have been used, then add vinegar until as sour as wished, but avoid thinning too much.

Oil should be kept in the dark and at a moderate temperature, sixty-five degrees to seventy-five degrees, to secure the best results.

SAUCE TARTARE

Is made by adding to the above fifteen drops onion juice, one teaspoonful capers, one teaspoonful gherkins, one teaspoonful parsley, each chopped exceedingly fine, one teaspoonful chervil if you have it.

SAUCE HOLLANDAISE.

Cook one tablespoonful flour in one teaspoonful butter, add slowly one cup strong veal or chicken stock; when it boils remove from the fire and whisk in the yolks of four eggs beaten smooth with one tablespoonful lemon juice and a few drops of onion juice, if liked; return to the fire and stir constantly till it begins to stiffen, then drop in one tablespoonful butter and beat with whisk till dissolved and smooth. It sounds like more trouble than it is, and is the best sauce made for boiled fish, cauliflower, asparagus, etc.

SAUCE FOR FRIED FISH OR FISH BALLS.

Two teaspoonfuls of dry mustard, one teaspoonful of flour, one teaspoonful of salt, one teaspoonful of soft butter, one teaspoonful of sugar, two tablespoonfuls of vinegar.

Mix in the order given, in a granite sauce pan; add one-half cup of boiling water and stir on the fire till it thickens and is smooth. Add two tablespoonfuls finely chopped pickles and serve it cold.

HORSE-RADISH BUTTER.

Pound in a mortar one teaspoonful of grated horse radish with one tablespoonful of butter. Season with one-third saltspoonful of red pepper. Rub through a fine sieve and keep in a cool place. When this butter is added to other sauces it should not boil again.

SHRIMP BUTTER.

Pick the meat from twelve cooked shrimp; dry the shells and pound altogether in a mortar adding one tablespoonful of good butter; place in a saucepan on a moderate fire, stirring until it clarifies, it will take about five minutes. Strain through a napkin pressing hard, and letting it drop into cold water. When it is hard, take it out and place in a warm bowl, stirring till it takes the desired color. Lobster butter is made in the same way.

HORSE-RADISH SAUCE.

One cup of freshly grated horse-radish, one teaspoonful salt, one-half saltspoonful pepper, one teaspoonful made mustard, two tablespoonfuls vinegar, well mixed together. Add one-half cup cream whipped very stiff.

BECHAMEL SAUCE.

One pint white stock, two tablespoonfuls butter, four tablespoonfuls flour, six mushrooms, or the liquor from a half can, one cup cream, one and a half tablespoonfuls lemon juice. Cook the butter and flour well together with salt and pepper if the stock is not already well seasoned. Add the stock as in plain white sauce, then the mushrooms, washed, peeled and cut small; let the sauce simmer twenty minutes with the lid half on. Skim off the butter as it rises. Strain through a fine sieve pressing hard; add the cream and lemon juice and let boil about three minutes. Pour out and stir often while cooling. If this is to be used to mask a chand-froid it will need one tablespoonful gelatine.

WELSH RAREBIT NO. 2.

Prepare six slices of toast, removing the crusts. Cut one pound of soft cheese in small bits and put them in a chafing-dish. Add one-half glass of ale or beer, one-half saltspoonful red pepper, and stir with a silver spoon until the whole mass is well melted. Serve the preparation on the toast which should already be on the plates.

WELSH RAREBIT AU GRATIN.

Prepare toast as in No. 2. Cover each slice with Swiss cheese, cut half inch thick. Lay them in a dripping-pan and dust lightly with pepper or spread made mustard over. Set in a hot oven till well melted, about ten minutes. The addition of a dropped egg to each slice makes what is called a Golden Buck.

DEVILED ALMONDS.

Blanch and shred two ounces almonds, fry to a light brown in butter, mix one tablespoonful of Chutney, two chopped gherkins, one tablespoonful Worcestershire sauce, one-quarter teaspoonful salt and a speck of cayenne well together, and toss the almonds in the mixture. Serve on croutons of fried bread.

COQUILLES OF OYSTER.

Blanch two dozen medium sized oysters in their own liquor for five minutes, add one-quarter saltspoonful pepper and one-half ounce butter; then drain them keeping the liquor for further use. Add the oysters to one-half pint velvet sauce, mix with three tablespoonfuls of the oyster liquor; keep it thick and be very careful not to break the oysters. Fill table shells with this preparation, cover with buttered crumbs and brown for five or six minutes in a very hot oven. Dress on a hot dish with a folded napkin and serve.

CROQUETTES OF MACARONI.

Boil one-quarter pound macaroni in salted water until very tender. Drain and toss in a saucepan with one heaped tablespoonful butter, one-half ounce Parmesan cheese, one-quarter ounce cooked tongue cut in fine dice. Spread on a well-buttered platter, about one inch thick, cover with a buttered paper, press it well down and set away to cool. Divide with the back of a knife into six parts, roll each one in grated cheese, then in beaten egg and in crumbs. Fry in very hot fat till well browned. Drain and serve on a folded napkin.

SALPICON ROYAL.

Cut a blanched sweetbread into small pieces and put them into a saucepan with one level tablespoonful of butter, six mushrooms and one truffle all cut into one-half inch dice. Add them to one-half pint of white sauce well seasoned with salt, pepper and a speck of nutmeg if liked. Let cook on a slow fire five minutes, tossing gently. Finish by adding one level tablespoonful shrimp butter, p. 111. Stir well and use to fill boucheés or for garnishing.

SALPICON OF LOBSTER.

One pint of good white sauce in a saucepan with four mushrooms, one truffle and one-quarter pint of diced lobster meat, that from the claw is the best. Thicken well by cooking five minutes, or add a liaison of two egg yolks and serve. The meat of three crawfish or six shrimps may be used instead of lobster.

COQUILLES OF CHICKEN, ENGLISH FASHION.

Fill six table-shells with a thick salpicon of chicken, mushrooms and truffles, made like the royal. Sprinkle the tops with grated bread crumbs well buttered. Bake a handsome brown in a very hot oven. Serve on a folded napkin.

CANAPÉ MADISON.

Prepare six medium sized slices of well-browned toast. Cover each with a very thin slice of lean cooked ham. Spread with a little made mustard, cover with a garnishing à la Provençale, dust a little grated Parmesan cheese over and strew buttered crumbs over all. Bake in a fiercely hot oven for six to eight minutes, or till well browned. Send to the table very hot, dressed on a hot dish with a folded napkin.

GARNISHING À LA PROVENÇALE.

Peel two solid white onions, mince them and parboil for five minutes; drain well and toss them in an omelet pan with one tablespoonful fresh butter for five minutes. Rub the spoon with a freshly cut clove of garlic, add a dash of lemon juice or white wine, one-half tablespoonful grated Parmesan cheese and one-half cup good white sauce. Season with salt and pepper. Stir all well until it comes to the boil, then set away to cool.

CHAUD-FROID OF CHICKEN.

Cut a cold-boiled chicken carefully into smooth joints, removing the skin. Mask each piece with Bechamel sauce, and arrange in a ring on a bed of lettuce. Mix sliced cucumber, diced beets and chopped tarragon with the heart-leaves of the lettuce and heap them in the centre. Served either with or without mayonnaise.

WHITE CURRY.

One fowl, one onion, two tablespoonfuls butter, two tablespoonfuls curry powder, two ounces sweet almonds, one-half teaspoonful salt, one-half tablespoonful lemon juice, one-half pint water. Cook the sliced onion in the butter till soft, but do not brown. Then add the fowl cut in very small pieces ready for serving. Sprinkle over the curry powder (most people would prefer half the quantity) and stir over the fire for five minutes. Blanch the almonds and pound them with a little water. When they are quite fine, put the remainder of the water to them and grind them well. Strain this through a strong strainer cloth pressing hard. It should come through looking like milk. Add this with salt to the fowl and simmer till tender; put in lemon juice just before serving. This is excellent made with veal. Grated cocoa-nut may take the place of almonds. Serve with rice.

ADDITIONAL RECIPES.

VEGETABLES.

French cooks very generally use carbonate of ammonia in cooking vegetables, to preserve the color. It is said to be harmless, as the ammonia all evaporates in boiling. A safe way is to allow a bit of bi-carbonate of soda, as large as a pea, to each quart of water, for all strong smelling vegetables, string beans, cauliflower, etc. It helps to make them tender, and relieves a little of the disagreeable smell, but the water should be changed for a few minutes before they are done, and a little salt added to the last water.

CAULIFLOWER.

Trim off outside leaves and lay blossoms down in cold salted water. Slugs and other insects will drop out, especially if gently shaken in the water. Tie in a piece of mosquito netting and lay in boiling salted water till very tender. Drain and serve with Hollandaise Sauce or Cream Sauce No. 1. This makes a delicious garnish for fried spring chicken or fried sweetbreads.

ARTICHOKES.

Trim closely, pare the under side, and cook in boiling water, with salt and a little vinegar. After they have cooked forty minutes, test by pulling out a leaf; if it detaches easily, it is done. Turn upside down on a sieve to drain. Serve with white, Bechamel or Hollandaise sauce. To keep them green, tie a bit of charcoal the size of an egg in a piece of cloth, and boil with them.

STUFFED EGG PLANT.

Choose a sound, smooth egg plant and drop into boiling water for ten minutes, then set to cool while preparing stuffing. One pint grated bread, one egg, two tablespoonfuls butter, one teaspoonful salt, one-half saltspoonful cayenne, one-half teaspoonful chopped onion, one teaspoonful chopped parsley. Cook onion and parsley in a large frying pan three minutes, then add one-half the bread crumbs. Divide the egg plant in two lengthwise, and with a spoon scoop out the greater part, leaving a shell nearly an inch thick. Chop this fine and add it to the bread crumb mixture in the frying pan. Cook the whole slowly, stirring often for ten or fifteen minutes. Remove from the fire, add the egg well beaten, and fill the shells, covering with remainder of the crumbs, and dotting with bits of butter. Bake in a hot oven twenty minutes, and serve very hot.

CELERY FRIED IN BATTER.

Take small roots, or divide large ones lengthwise; trim the root portion smooth, and cut the stalks down to four or five inches long. Cook ten minutes in boiling salted water, dry quickly on a thick towel. Dip them in fritter batter and fry a good brown in deep hot fat. Drain on soft paper, arrange on a folded napkin and send to the table with grated cheese.

POTATO CROQUETTES.

Season cold mashed potatoes with salt and pepper, a little nutmeg; beat to a cream, with a tablespoonful of melted butter to every cupful of potatoes, add two beaten eggs and some chopped parsley. Roll into small balls, dip in egg and milk, coat them with cracker dust, and fry in hot lard. S.

CORN FRITTERS.

Beat an egg light and add to it one-half cup of milk, pour this mixture upon one cup of flour and beat well; then add one teaspoonful salt, a little pepper and a spoon of melted butter, mix well, add one-half can of corn, chopped very fine, drop by spoonfuls into boiling lard and cook about three minutes. S.

PARSNIP FRITTERS.

Boil five parsnips until tender, take off the skins and mash very fine, add one teaspoonful of flour, one egg, a little salt,

Make the mixture into small cakes with a spoon. Fry them on both sides to a delicate brown and serve hot. S.

VERMICELLI CAKES.

Bring one quart of water to boil and drop one pound of vermicelli into the boiling water, stir well and strain when tender through a sieve; then add one cup of flour, two teaspoonfuls Star Crystal Baking Powder, the yolks of three eggs, one-half cup of melted butter, beat the whites of the eggs to a very stiff froth, mix thoroughly and bake in hot oven. S.

MACARONI AU GRATIN.

Take one-half pound of pipe macaroni, seven ounces of cheese, four ounces of butter, one pint of fresh milk, one quart of water, and some bread crumbs. Flavor milk and water with a pinch of nutmeg and salt, set over the fire and when boiling drop in the macaroni. When tender drain it from the milk and water, put it into a deep dish, sprinkle some of the grated cheese on top, pour the remainder over it and bake to a nice brown. S.

BRUSSELS SPROUTS.

Cut the sprouts from two medium-sized stalks, pick off all tarnished leaves and lay them for an hour in salted water. Drain them well and cook in plenty of boiling water uncovered till tender, from ten minutes to half an hour, according to their age. Drain in a colander and serve with a Bechamel or Hollandaise sauce.

SPRING CARROTS.

Wash and scrape them, parboil for ten minutes and dry them on a cloth. Return to the saucepan with one heaped tablespoonful sugar, one cup stock, one tablespoonful butter, and boil gently about half an hour or until perfectly tender then remove the cover and boil fast until the stock is reduced to glaze. Sprinkle with a little chopped parsley and serve with the glaze on them.

ASPARAGUS.

Wash carefully two bunches green asparagus, cut the ends until the tender part is reached. Arrange in one large bundle and fasten with a broad band of coarse muslin, pinned at each side. Boil gently in salted water until done, about twenty minutes. Serve with Hollandaise sauce.

ASPARAGUS AU POIS.

Cut the tender part in bits as long as the stems are thick and boil till tender. Drain and add to two bunches one-half cup cream, one-quarter teaspoonful salt. Simmer till reduced to a thick sauce and serve like green peas.

BROILED CÈPES.

Open the can and pour off the oil. Drop the cèpes into hot water to cleanse them from the oil and dry them on a soft cloth. Season with salt and pepper, brush them with melted butter and roll in flour. Broil for six minutes over a hot fire. Place each on a round of toast, pour over a little melted butter and lemon juice and serve at once.

STEWED CÈPES.

Free from oil as before and cut into cubes. For a pint can use three tablespoonfuls butter, one tablespoonful flour, one tablespoonful lemon juice, one teaspoonful salt, one teaspoonful onion juice, a dust of pepper and one-half pint stock. Melt the butter and add the cèpes and flour. Stir until a light coffee brown, then add the stock and seasonings and set back to simmer five minutes. If this is to be served as an entreé, arrange on toast; but they make a delicious garnish for broiled fish.

MUSHROOMS.

Mushrooms are often plenty in the fields during the summer and fall, and are far superior in delicacy and flavor to the cultivated ones, but they should be used while fresh. Cut off and throw away the stems, pare the tops and throw them into a bowl with plenty of water with a little vinegar. Use a silver knife and if the vegetables do not blacken the silver they are safe to use.

STEWED MUSHROOMS.

Cut them in small bits after draining from the acidulated water and for each pint allow a generous tablespoonful of butter, one-half teaspoonful salt and a speck of pepper, just enough water to keep them from sticking to the sauce pan, simmer for ten minutes, or, use one-half cup of cream instead of water and serve on toast.

BROILED MUSHROOMS.

Select large ones with deep cups. Place over clear coals cup side down first and cook two minutes, then turn and cook two minutes on the other side, remove carefully not to spill the juice and serve on buttered toast, sprinkle with salt and pepper and lay a bit of butter on each.

BAKED MUSHROOMS.

Lay them in a baking dish cup side up. Fill the cups with any kind of chopped and seasoned meat. Cover with buttered crumbs and bake in a very hot oven ten to fifteen minutes.

LENTILS.

Wash and soak one pint of lentils over night. In the morning drain and cover with fresh warm water adding one-quarter teaspoonful bi-carbonate of soda. Boil gently till they begin to grow tender (probably about two hours). Change them to fresh water, adding one teaspoonful salt and cook till they break at the least touch. Drain in a colander. Put two tablespoonfuls butter in a frying pan; when melted add the lentils with salt and pepper to taste; toss over the fire for fifteen minutes. Delicious served with cold meat for lunch.

POTATOES

Should always be peeled before boiling except while very young and delicate. If they are not mealy, wrap each one in a strong crash towel as soon as done and wring the towel as hard as possible. Untwist the towel and roll out as carefully as possible onto a hot dish. When broken with a fork, these will fall into a mass of meal almost like starch.

POTATOES AU GRATIN.

Steam them until done, cut in slices one-eighth of an inch thick and arrange in a heated dish seasoning each layer. Pour over an equal bulk of thin Bechamel sauce and bake in a very hot oven till brown.

FRIED POTATOES.

Cut cold boiled potatoes in slices and season with salt and pepper. Have frying pan hot with just enough dripping to cover the bottom. Brown the slices on both sides and keep hot till all are fried. These are a delightful garnish for breakfast ham.

FRIED POTATOES, FRENCH.

Pare the potatoes and throw into cold water for at least an hour. Cut in slices, blocks, strips, balls or any fancy shape, and dry them on a towel. Drop quickly into fat hot enough to brown them by the time they come to the surface. They are done when they float. Skim into a draining basket and set in the oven to keep hot. Sprinkle with salt and serve hot, either as a garnish or for a vegetable.

PLANTATION SWEET POTATOES.

Cut cold cooked sweet potatoes in rather thick slices. Put them in a deep dish with pepper, salt and butter, pour on a little milk, enough to barely show between the pieces, and bake in a moderate oven one hour.

BOILED SALSIFY.

Wash, scrape and throw into cold water. Cut into inch pieces and boil rapidly uncovered in a granite stew-pan. A little vinegar will help to keep it white. Drain them well and serve with plenty of butter and lemon juice, salt and pepper to taste.

SALSIFY FRITTERS

Are made like parsnip fritters.

FRIED TOMATOES.

Wipe and cut in halves as many as you need, dip the cut side of each half in fine bread crumbs that have been well seasoned with pepper, salt and sugar, place them in a buttered granite baking-pan, skin side down. Drop bits of butter between them and stand over a moderate fire to fry very slowly, turning as soon as brown. When they are tender take them up carefully with a cake turner and slide them onto a heated platter. Draw the baking-pan forward, and when the butter is a nice brown, add two tablespoonfuls flour, mix smooth, pour in one pint milk or cream, stirring steadily until it boils. Add more seasoning if needed and pour around the tomatoes.

ADDITIONAL RECIPES.

COOKING FOR INVALIDS.

QUICKLY MADE BEEF TEA.

Broil a slice of round steak for one minute on each side. Lay on a deep plate and score very closely, cutting only one-half the way through. Turn and score the other side at right angles with the first. Pour over hot water to half cover the meat. Set in a warm place and turn and press with a fork often for ten minutes. Squeeze the meat dry, add salt to taste and more water if too strong to be agreeable. It must not be allowed to get too hot or it will turn gray and be full of coagulated albumen.

BEEF TEA NO. 2.

Cut three-quarter pound lean beef from the round into thin slices; soak for thirty minutes or as much longer as you have time, add in one pint of cold soft water, stirring and squeezing occasionally. Set over fire and simmer for ten minutes. Strain, season with salt and serve hot.

BEEF TEA NO. 3.

Cut one pound lean beef in half inch bits, put them into a glass jar, set the jar on a stand in a kettle of cold water; bring it to a boil and let boil slowly for three to four hours, strain, and if there is the least particle of the fat remove it by laying tissue paper lightly on the surface. This can be used clear or diluted with water to the taste.

CHICKEN BROTH.

Cut up a fowl and crack the bones. Put into three pints of cold water and bring slowly to the boiling point. Simmer closely covered for three to four hours, or until the meat all falls apart.

Strain it and let cool to remove the fat if you have time, if it is needed in a hurry skim off as much as possible and remove the last atoms with tissue paper. Salt to taste and for each pint of liquor allow one tablespoonful of rice that has been soaked an hour in tepid water. Simmer until the rice is perfectly soft, about twenty minutes, and send pepper (if allowed) and crisp crackers to the invalid with it.

Young chickens should never be chosen for broth as they are much less nutritious and highly flavored than a fowl a year or more old.

MUTTON BROTH.

This is made in the same way, allowing one quart of cold water to each pound of meat and bone. The neck and shoulders are the best pieces for broth.

VEAL BROTH.

This may be given to a convalescent for a change, but is neither as digestible or nourishing as beef. It is much improved by cooking in it one tablespoonful Pearl tapioca for each pint of broth and adding one-half cupful of cream just before serving.

BROILED CHOPS.

A steak or chop for an invalid should be broiled over a fire of charcoal, if practicable, as that leaves no flavor of smoke or gas on the meat; where that is not possible the meat should be folded in a sheet of well-buttered, glossy writing paper and the edges folded together like the edges of a turnover. Lift from the fire often lest the paper burn, and allow a few minutes longer than when directly over the coals. When done, cut a slit in the folded side of paper, and slide the meat and gravy together unto a hot plate.

FILLETS OF FISH.

These may be broiled in the same way and are much more juicy than when broiled in an open grid iron. Spread with a little soft butter, sprinkle on lemon juice, chopped parsley, salt and pepper and set in oven a few minutes before serving. Dark meat and game are generally more easily digested as well as more nourishing and should therefore be chosen for invalids and convalescents.

CODFISH IN CREAM.

Shred one-quarter cupful of salt fish and cover well with tepid water, let it stand while making one-half pint of cream sauce No. 1 on p. 109, drain the fish carefully, add it to the sauce, and as soon it comes to the boiling point serve with baked potatoes.

CODFISH IN CREAM NO. 2.

Cut salt fish in one-quarter inch dice, pour boiling water over it and let stand for five minutes. Allow one cup of thin cream to one-quarter cup of fish, drain the fish, add to the boiling cream and serve on toast. A speck of cayenne is a great improvement.

OATMEAL GRUEL.

Roll one-half cup of coarse oat meal until very mealy; put into a large tumbler and fill with water, stir it well, let it settle a moment and than pour off all but the bran, repeat until three waters have been used. Bring the water to a boil as quickly as possible and cook twenty minutes, stirring often, add salt to taste and thin with milk, cream or beef tea.

CORNMEAL GRUEL.

One quart of water, boiling, one teaspoonful salt, mix two tablespoonfuls cornmeal and one tablespoonful of flour with one-half cupful of cold water. Pour it into the boiling salted water, stirring briskly. Simmer, covered, an hour, strain and serve with milk or cream.

MILK PORRIDGE.

One pint of boiling milk, one tablespoonful of flour, mixed smooth with one-half cupful of cold milk and one saltspoonful of salt, stir into the hot milk and cook in double boiler one-half hour. If allowed, a handful of raisins cut in quarters and a bit of nutmeg one-half as large as a pea, may be boiled in the milk. Strain before serving.

BREAD GRUEL.

One cupful of coarsely grated stale bread, simmered in one pint of water till almost dissolved. Strain and salt to taste. The addition of beef essence or milk or cream must depend upon the patient but it is palatable and nutritious served plain.

EGG NOG.

One egg beaten to a cream, one teaspoonful of sugar, speck of salt, one-half cup of milk, one tablespoonful of wine. Mix in order given and stir well.

WINE WHEY.

One cup of new milk heated to boiling point, add one-half wine-glass full of good sherry or any wine that is not sweet. Boil a minute, strain and use with or without sugar. In cases of nausea, pour it into a glass half full of chipped ice, and give a teaspoonful at a time with the ice.

MULLED WINE.

One pint of sherry, one and a half cups of water set to boil, while beating to a cream the yolks of six eggs, with one scant cup of sugar, one-quarter nutmeg, grated.

Whip the whites to a stiff froth and whisk them into the yolks, pour on the boiling wine, beating constantly; pour back and forth until cool enough to serve.

KOUMISS.

Dissolve a third of a one-ounce cake of compressed yeast, or its equivalent of fluid yeast in a little warm, not hot water. Take a quart of milk fresh from the cow, or warmed to blood heat, and add to it one tablespoonful of sugar, and the dissolved yeast. Put the mixture in beer bottles with patent stoppers, fill to the neck and let stand for twelve hours at a temperature of 75 or 80 degrees. Then put the bottles on ice, upside down until wanted. Be careful to keep the bottle turned upside down.

TOAST WATER.

Toast two slices of bread as brown as possible without burning. Break into a pitcher and while hot pour on one quart of cold water. It is ready for use in one-half hour.

PANADA.

Lay in a bowl one Boston cracker split; sprinkle on a pinch of salt and cover with boiling water. Set the bowl into boiling water and let stand until the cracker looks clear, about one-half hour. Drain off the water and slide into a hot saucer without breaking. Eat with sugar and cream. They are good only when very hot and fresh.

PARCHED RICE.

Roast to a good brown like coffee, then cook as usual and eat with syrup or sugar and cream.

HERB TEAS.

For the dried herbs allow one teaspoonful to a cup of boiling water. Cover and stand where they will not boil for from 5 to 10 minutes. Strain before serving. Too long steeping makes them bitter or acrid without increasing the medicinal value.

ADDITIONAL RECIPES.

Things Good to Know.

HOW TO BUTTER AND ROLL BREAD.

Cut all the crust from a loaf of fresh bread. Cream, with a fork, enough butter to make as many rolls as needed. Spread thin on one end of the loaf; with a thin sharp knife, cut the thinnest possible slice. Roll this slice, buttered side inward and lay on a napkin. When the napkin is full, draw it firmly around the rolls and pin it in shape, lay in a cold damp place for several hours. The rolls will keep their shape without tying.

HOW TO DISSOLVE GELATINE.

If gelatine be covered with warm water and set in a warm place it will melt in fifteen or twenty minutes, but will develop the strong flavor of glue and spoil whatever it is added to.

A better way is to allow one cup cold water for two ounces (one package) of gelatine and let it soak until perfectly soft. Cox's make will require two hours, Nelson's or Andrews' will be soft in from fifteen to thirty minutes, then add a little boiling liquid stirring till all is dissolved, and the rest of the liquid should be added cold. Gelatine never dissolves in cold water but only absorbs a certain amount. If water is left it can be drained away without taking any goodness from the gelatine.

HOW TO KILL A LOBSTER.

When a live lobster is required for broiling or other purposes run a long, narrow bladed knife into the tail at the third joint from the end, slanting the blade downward. This cuts the spinal cord and death will quickly follow, but it should be cooked at once.

TO RELIEVE A BURN.

Wet with cold water and cover with bi-carbonate of soda, bind a cloth around and keep damp until free from pain.

IF FAT BOILS OVER.

Lift off the kettle instantly to stop the supply, open all the dampers and covers of the stove to draw the flames and smoke into the chimney. If the blazing fat runs over on the floor throw on ashes or sand, *never water*, which only scatters the flame. Where much frying is done a box of sand should be kept close by the stove.

RED and black ants may be effectually driven away by using Persian Insect Powder, sprinkled wherever they intrude. It is perfectly harmless to man or beast and deadly poison to insects. To destroy flies and mosquitoes with it, burn it by sprinkling it over live coals or by heaping it on a plate and setting it on fire.

A MIXTURE of one pound of powdered charcoal and four pounds plaster of Paris, sprinkled under porches or in damp corners, will prove a good disinfectant.

IF a few trays of charcoal are set in a damp cellar where milk is kept, there will be no danger of the milk becoming tainted.

IF a cellar has its windows closed by day and open at night, it will not be damp.

BY placing a dish containing a good-sized lump of unslacked lime, in a refrigerator, the moisture will be absorbed, so removing all danger from mould.

WHITE lead will cement broken crockery better than anything else. Apply a brush to each edge, press together and set aside for a few days. Water has no effect on it.

A HEATED knife will cut hot bread without making it soggy.

OXALIC acid, dissolved in hot water, will clean paint from windows.

BROOMS dipped in boiling suds once a week for a few minutes will last much longer than they otherwise would. Paint brushes, bristle brooms, camels hair brushes, etc., will not shed their bristles if allowed to soak in water and dried slowly.

KID shoes may be kept soft and free from cracks if rubbed once a week with pure glycerine or castor oil.

A PIECE of zinc placed on the coals of a hot stove will clean out the stove pipe.

RATS detest chloride of lime and coal tar.

STONE jars that have become unfit for use from any cause can be purified by filling with fresh earth and allowing it to remain two or three weeks.

A CRASH bag wet with ammonia water and drawn over a broom enables one to freshen the carpet of the living room every morning without dust; it is also very nice to use on any carpet after a thorough sweeping to remove the dust that settles.

COTTON batting is impervious to all life germs. Draw it carefully over a full jar of preserved fruit and it will prevent mould and fermentation.

VINEGAR is better than ice for keeping fish. By putting a little vinegar on the fish it will keep perfectly well even in hot weather. Fish is often improved in flavor under this treatment.

To bake batter cakes on a common griddle without grease or smoke, add a teaspoonful of melted lard to every quart of batter, just before you begin to bake. Put your griddle on the stove, put some salt on; when it gets hot, rub off well with a piece of brown paper. You will have to repeat the salting if, after you stop baking, you let the griddle stand on the stove.

HOW TO KEEP SUET.

Select the nicest looking suet, as free as possible from veins or spots; have your pot just near enough to the fire to melt the suet very gradually; pour it into a vessel of very cold clear water as soon as it is melted, it will soon grow quite firm, wipe all dampness from it, cover it with the waxed paper used by confectioners, if it can possibly be got, otherwise use any white paper. Envelop it in linen, and keep dry and cool.   S.

POLISH FOR HARDWOOD FLOORS AND FURNITURE.

One quarter pound beeswax, 1 ounce castile soap, turpentine to soften. Shave the soap very fine and dissolve in turpentine. Insert a tin with wax and some turpentine in a vessel of boiling water, and keep adding turpentine until well dissolved. Allow plenty of time. Fully a quart of turpentine will be needed. Make of consistency of soft jelly, adding at the last one tablespoonful sweet oil. Apply a very little at a time, with canton flannel, and polish with a soft cloth.

TO PROTECT A STOVE FROM RUST WHEN STORED.

One-half gallon benzine, three-fourths pound pulverized rosin.

TO KEEP STOCKINGS FROM FADING.

Let them soak in hot salt water until water is cold. Thoroughly rinse.

TO CLEAN CARPET.

One bar of white ivory soap, cut in fine shavings and boil in one gallon of water until melted. Add four ounces of borax, four ounces of sal soda. Stir 5 minutes, and add four gallons of cold soft water and one-half pint of alcohol.

FURNITURE POLISH NO. 1.

One-third linseed oil, one-third turpentine, one-third vinegar. Rub on with flannel, polish with either flannel or chamois. First wash the article with strong castile suds.

FURNITURE POLISH NO. 2.

Take equal parts of sweet oil and vinegar, mix, add one pint of gum arabic, finely powdered. This will make furniture look almost as good as new, and can be easily applied, as it requires no rubbing. The bottle should be shaken and the polish poured on a rag and applied to the furniture.   S.

TO CLEAN WALL PAPER.

Equal parts of soft water and ammonia, thickened with rye flour till stiff as putty. Make into a ball and rub over any wall paper, except velvet surfaces.

RECEIPT FOR SILVER WASH.

One ounce of nitric acid, one ten cent piece and one ounce of quick silver, put in an open glass vessel and let it stand until dissolved, then add one pint of water and it is ready for use; make it into a powder by adding whiting and it may be used on brass, copper, german silver, etc.   S.

WASHING FLUID.

One pound of sal soda, one pound of unslacked lime, four quarts soft water. Boil all together in any kettle but an iron one; when cold and clear, pour off and put in a stone jug. Put one-half cup in water and rub the clothes on the soiled places. Soap well; put into your boiler one cup of the mixture with sufficient cold water to cover the clothes, boil ten or fifteen minutes, rinse thoroughly, rubbing them if necessary.

In case of sickness the bedding can be thrown into the boiler into which the mixture has been put, having the water boiling hot, taking care to wet them in cold water first.

Consider:

That you cannot buy silk at the price of cotton.
That gold dollars cannot be had for sixty cents.
That diamonds are worth more than paste.
That cheap goods are the most costly in the end.
That impure ingredients produce poor results.
That pure ingredients produce good results.
That the best is always the cheapest.
That cream tartar is worth more than alum.
That Flint's Star Crystal Baking Powder is absolutely pure.
That it does not contain either alum or ammonia.
That it is a straight cream tartar powder.
That it is of full value in itself and requires no gift enterprises to help sell it.
When you are buying baking powder buy *it*, when you want trinkets buy *them*, they will not help your cooking.

Every article put up by me and branded pure is **strictly pure,** and so guaranteed. By using my pure coffees and spices you get the best, and therefore make no mistake.

J. G. FLINT.

www.ingramcontent.com/pod-product-compliance
Lightning Source LLC
Chambersburg PA
CBHW020102170426
43199CB00009B/367